WIFE OF A SOLDIER, A JOURNEY OF FAITH

Diana Juergens

PublishAmerica
Baltimore

First printing

Softcover 1-60610-006-8
Hardcover 978-1-4489-1367-1
PAperback 978-1-4512-6729-7
PUBLISHED BY PUBLISHAMERICA, LLLP
www.publishamerica.com
Baltimore

Printed in the United States of America

Foreword

This is a book about my Lord, my wife, my children, and my profession. At times in the following pages it may seem as if I am some kind of hero. The reality could not be farther from the truth. I am an average guy married to an incredible woman. The real hero of this story is my wife Diana and the Lord who is at work in her life. My children are heroes too. They have lived through the deployments and separations. Instead of just surviving, they have prospered.

As I write, we are again in the midst of a long separation. As we were preparing for this time apart, we had the opportunity to relocate anywhere in the US or stay in our beachfront condo that had been our home for the previous ten months while I attended the Joint War College. Yet we decided to move to a nearby Army Post so that Diana and our children could stay involved in the military community and help others who experience the demands that confront military families.

It is amazing to watch all that is happening as the Lord uses difficult situations to draw us closer to Him and to impact the world. This book is a story about a family's journey of faith. It's the story of imperfect people empowered by a mighty God. It's a story about life lived to the fullest for the glory of the Lord. I pray that it is a blessing to you.

Rich Juergens
Soto Cano, Honduras
15 Jan 2009

ACKNOWLEDGEMENTS

Thanks to my mother-in-law, Gail Juergens, for giving of her time to read and reread my chapters, helping me to make my message clear.

Thanks to my prayer warriors, my eight daughters, for believing in me, speaking words of encouragement, and claiming that this book would one day be a reality. A special thanks to my third daughter, Mary, for selflessly giving of her time and investing countless hours on the computer to get this work to the final stages. Without her help, it would never have been possible.

Thanks to my husband, for choosing me to be his wife. I am very grateful for his willingness and courage to speak the challenging words to me as this project was in the working stages. I thank him for his support, patience, and love.

And to the Lord, my Savior, Redeemer, Father, and my intimate friend, who holds my heart in His hands. Without His unconditional love for me, my life would have been without purpose. May He be glorified by the simple words of my testimony written throughout this book! It was by His leading that this project began. May He use it to bring a message of encouragement and hope.

CHAPTER 1

FOUNDATION OF FAITH, A TIME OF SURRENDER

Commit your way to the Lord, trust also in Him,
and He shall bring it to pass.
Psalm 37:5

In early June 1985 a young, newly commissioned lieutenant arrived at the Army's aviator training post at Fort Rucker, Alabama. She had an intensity that few understood. As the top cadet in the ROTC program in her university she had her pick of military careers to pursue. She chose aviation with plans to add helicopter pilot to her list of accomplishments.

There were several things she knew for sure. She knew that she could do anything a man could do, and in most cases, do it better. She knew that she would never put herself in a position of dependence on anyone, especially a man. Her mom had taught her that lesson. She knew that she had a life of adventure ahead, serving her country and traveling to exciting places. Her journey was just beginning, with trails to blaze and a lot to prove.

I was that lieutenant with the independent, strong, prideful, hard heart. And while I believed that my journey had just begun, and that I was on the road to success, God had different, yet much better plans for me.

I was excited to see a familiar face as I spotted Rich. Only three months before, I had sat next to him at the George Marshall Conference, a gathering of the top cadets from across the nation. I remember glancing at him when our national anthem had finished playing and seeing teary eyes through my own blurry ones and thinking, "Wow! He loves his country with a passion just like me." Two months later, we were standing side by side once again. This time it was in our platoon at the Officer Basic Course at Fort Rucker, Alabama. My weekends were filled with studying and church. On Sundays, I continued in the tradition of my small Wisconsin farming community upbringing and attended Lutheran services at the post chapel. The congregation consisted of a small group of families and me. On Mondays, Rich came to class with wonderful stories from his church service and his singles Sunday school class. The stories wouldn't end there. He would come on other days of the week sharing about Wednesday evening service and the friendly people he had met who included him in their lives. Hayrides and potlucks were just a few of the fun events that caught my attention. When he said he had been invited to someone's home for a meal I was impressed. To a soldier away from home, this was a big deal!

Rich often invited those of us in the platoon to join him for church. After weeks of his friendly but persistent pestering I agreed to give it a try. This decision changed the course of my life forever. The very first Sunday, in the singles Sunday school class, I experienced something I had never allowed myself to feel before: the genuine love of Christ. People who did not know me took the time to ask me all about myself, my family, and how I was enjoying Alabama. They made me feel not only welcomed, but accepted and loved. They had something that I knew I wanted. And, they knew something I had been searching for since I was sixteen and my dad died unexpectedly. They understood the real meaning and purpose of life. I found out that they not only believed in salvation through Jesus Christ, but they had also surrendered their wants and desires to what God wanted in their lives. In the course of one week, after reading the book of John, I went from knowing about God, to believing I absolutely needed Him to forgive me and take control of my heart and life. October 1985 began my personal walk with the Lord, a journey on which He immediately began to transform my heart and mind. Needless to say, Rich and I began to spend a lot of time together as we attended the same Sunday school class and church. We got very involved in helping with the youth program, which God used to draw me closer to Him.

The young kids in the group challenged me because they knew more about the Bible than I did. I began to get up extra early, sometimes as early as 4:00 AM, to read my Bible before going to class or the flight line. Without a doubt that investment of time had the most significant impact on my life the whole year I spent at Fort Rucker.

I joined the Army for three reasons: I wanted to serve my country, travel to Europe and become independent, so that I would never have to trust any man to take care of me! Marriage was NOT in my plans. Instead, an army career was my goal! God began to work on this immediately. He softened my heart, and I began to realize how much I really "liked" my good friend Rich. Rich was a man unlike any other I had ever met before. I admired his steadfast faith in God and his heart to please God in all that he did. Rich was a man of integrity. Our time together began side by side in the same squad in our Officers Basics Course. We began to admire one another's character as we were physically pushed to the limit. A friendship and bond grew between us as we worked together with the rest of our platoon to accomplish the tasks set before us. The last week was spent in the field. I now joke with our daughters and tell them that Dad fell in love with me even after that week without a shower, matted-down hair, and a camouflaged face.

I began flight school in October 1985. My first day in the aircraft found me experiencing a curious mix of excitement and fear. As my instructor pilot and I buckled into our seats, he said, "I do something every day before I fly. You can join me or just listen." He began to pray and ask for God's protection and wisdom as we flew that day. I was amazed. God had given me an instructor pilot who loved Him and trusted Him for all the areas of his life. I experienced a touch of God's love that day as well as His sense of humor! From that day on, I knew God really loved me and was in control of my life.

Once flight school started, Rich and I spent time together regularly on the weekends. By spring we knew our relationship had grown into something more than just a friendship; however, we both had our army goals. Rich requested that we begin to pray about our future assignments. He suggested that we both put down our first choices on our assignment sheets. I agreed, so he put down Panama and I put down Germany. He said, "If God wants us together, He will open the door."

I certainly had mixed emotions when I heard his idea. My first thought was, "There is no way God could answer such a prayer," and my second was, "I have surrendered my heart and now the love of my life is going to Panama and I am going to Germany. What have I gotten myself into now?"

As you may have guessed, God DID answer, as we both received orders for Fort Lewis, Washington! This was enough to prove to me that God cares about the details of our lives. Rich proposed to me as he traveled back for my flight school graduation in July 1986. We went on to Fort Lewis in September 1986, with plans to be married the following June. As two young army aviators, we were assigned to the same brigade but to different battalions. We both were driven and committed to doing our very best. We worked many long hours and hardly ever saw each other. We had found a good church and we also found a home we wanted to buy. We changed our plans and began marriage counseling with our pastor. Once finished, he asked when we would like to be married. Rich said, "How about next Sunday night?" We were married on November 16, 1986, at the beginning of a special Sunday night worship service. We were able to live in our new home and begin building our marriage relationship in the midst of our intense lifestyle. God's plan for my life was in motion, with two new companions and loves, the Lord and my husband.

Our military careers continued to demand much of our time. We both loved flying helicopters in the Army, leading soldiers, and getting to know them and their families. On top of that, in the spring of 1987, I was chosen as one of very few pilots to attend the highly sought-after UH60 Blackhawk Qualification Course at Fort Rucker, Alabama, scheduled to begin in July. I was thrilled and couldn't wait to get there. A few weeks before I left, I came down with the flu, or so I thought. My husband immediately said, "You're pregnant!" I was in complete denial.

The Lord surprised us with our first blessing, Elizabeth Jean. A good part of the pregnancy, I tried to stay angry because of how it would affect my career. Yet, as time went on, the pregnancy began to soften my heart. On February 29, 1988, the moment I held my new baby girl, I immediately began to question my career goals. God used my little girl to begin transforming my heart to the call of motherhood.

I spent the next two and a half years trying to do it all. The world says a woman can do it: have a successful career, a great marriage, and wonderful children. Experiencing it for myself proved to me that despite my best efforts, something would suffer as I tried to do it all. For me, physically, I suffered severe headaches because of the stresses of work and the crazy schedule. I also began to resent my husband, who never had to take the baby to the doctor or stay up all night when she was sick, and then try to function at work and to make up the work missed.

From the beginning, God provided close friends who volunteered to care for Elizabeth while I worked. I was very thankful yet deep down it tormented me to know she spent more time with them each week than she did with me. Bottom line, Elizabeth was being raised by someone else. I began to feel that was not God's heart for our marriage or our little girl. God again began to challenge me in a new and unexpected area, getting out of the service.

This became a real battle for me. I loved what I did and I had worked hard to become a soldier. I spent months talking with God about all the reasons why I felt I should be able to stay in the Army. Patiently God waited and loved me as I wrestled with His call to end my career in the military and begin a new one as a full-time wife and mom.

As I wrestled with my decision, a huge temptation was brought into my life. Whether it was a test from God or a plot of the enemy, I am still uncertain, but it definitely made my decision that much harder. My battalion commander offered me a company command. Company command is the dream of every young officer and I was to be the first woman company commander in the history of my aviation battalion. My wise husband never said a word. He knew I was going to have to continue to seek God and ultimately make the final decision to stay in the Army or resign my commission myself.

God was ever so patient with me. My heart began to hurt each morning as I dropped off my Elizabeth, now two, to spend the day with someone else. As it got harder and harder, I would drive to work with tears rolling down my face. Finally, one morning it became too unbearable for my heart as her mother to leave her. I had to ask God to help me with my fear. I was afraid that if I got out, Elizabeth would long to stay with my friend instead of with me. I was finally able to surrender my career after confessing my fear to God.

After dropping off Elizabeth, I went straight to my battalion commander's office and told him I would be submitting my resignation. He looked me straight in the eyes and said, "Diana, you are an outstanding army officer but I don't know how you have managed to 'do it all' this long."

I expected to have to defend my position, yet God had already put it into the heart of my battalion commander to support and encourage me in my decision. I felt his reaction was confirmation that I had truly heard the Lord and He wanted me home. I put in my resignation just a few months before the Iraqi invasion of Kuwait and the start of Operation Desert Shield. At the time I was the battalion adjutant. I was responsible for all of the personal action paperwork submitted by the soldiers within our battalion. As I waited for the answer on my own resignation, I watched many other soldiers' resignations come back denied even though our paperwork had been submitted prior to the invasion.

I continued to be hopeful and prayed that God would still allow me to get out of the service. I could not imagine leaving my two-and-a-half-year-old daughter. As aviators in the same brigade I knew, if required, my husband and I would be deployed to Iraq.

Eventually, my paperwork did come back approved. I believe God had moved in the heart of someone in the Pentagon on my behalf. He had heard the cry of my heart and I believe He honored my prayers as I obeyed His voice to give up my career and get out of the service, to take care of our young family.

The day I signed out of the Army was the same day we left Fort Lewis for our next duty assignment at Fort Rucker, Alabama. It was as if God allowed me to drive away from my old call into my new one: a full-time military wife and mother. I had the best of both worlds. I had served my country as a soldier and would now be able to use my experience to be the

13

best military spouse I could be. The desire of my heart became one of supporting my husband, a warrior in the service of our country, and to be available to care for the needs of our children myself.

We currently have eight beautiful daughters. Each has a passionate love for God. We are in our twenty-third year of military service and our twenty-second year of marriage. I say "we" because "we" represents the sacrifice of the whole family to support our soldier. Both our marriage and active duty service require a wholehearted commitment to be successful! I love and appreciate my husband much more now than the day I said "I do." I am also more passionate than ever to embrace this military lifestyle. I am so grateful for the daughters God has given us. They are a daily reminder of God's perfect plan. They too have embraced this lifestyle and see it as an opportunity to serve their country by supporting their dad. If I had chosen to stay in the military, I know our Elizabeth would have been an only child and my path in life would have looked very different. The result of my willingness to obey God's leading eighteen years ago has been the unfolding of God's absolute best plan for my life.

CHAPTER 2
THE COMMITMENT TO SUPPORT MY MAN OF VALOR

"I heard the voice of the Lord saying: 'Whom
shall I send and who will go for us?" And I said,
'Here am I, send me.'
Isaiah 6:8

We are in this together…a God-given call on my life was
taking hold of my heart that would bring blessings and
challenges.

The day I signed out of the Army, Rich, our two-and-half-
year-old Elizabeth, our two dogs and I departed Washington
State in a two-vehicle convoy. In the lead vehicle were my
father-in-law and his brother Fred. Both had volunteered to
drive our truck across country so Rich, Elizabeth and I could
ride together. We were headed back to Fort Rucker, Alabama,
where Rich would attend his Advance Course. I was six weeks
pregnant with our second daughter, Hannah, and was

experiencing extreme morning sickness. Worse than the sickness was the fear I felt as I entered a new phase of life.

I was a well-trained army helicopter pilot. I had been the operations officer for an aviation company. The responsibilities for planning and deploying up to twenty helicopters and executing operations for a wide variety of missions fell on my shoulders. I had also been the battalion S-1 or adjutant for eighteen months. I managed all personnel matters in a battalion with 650 soldiers. You would think I could handle the responsibility of one soldier and a toddler, but I was scared because I was not trained to run a home.

I also realized that during four years of marriage, I had competed with my husband instead of making our marriage stronger by being his support and completing him. My commitment to our marriage and the Army had been mostly about me as I focused on my own career and goals. While I went through the motions of attending Family Readiness Group (FRG) meetings for my husband's unit, my heart was not in it. As I began to see how important my attitude toward my husband and his chosen profession was, I realized I had a decision to make. Was I going to commit my whole heart to God's plan for my life, which included embracing this military lifestyle He had placed me in? Was I willing to make the commitment to wholeheartedly support my husband in his career and the people that would be placed in my life as a military spouse?

I kept reminding myself that God called me home to be a support for my husband and our family. As confirmation He had made it happen during a period of time when the nation was preparing for war in Iraq. My resignation had been approved in the midst of the buildup for Desert Storm. It was miraculous! James 4:15 says, "If the Lord wills, we shall live to do this or that." I knew the Lord wanted me to be a full-time wife and mother yet I felt inadequate for the job. I began to pray earnestly for God's help and confessed my needs to a few close friends, asking them to pray for me.

Now that I was ready to receive Godly counsel, God began to answer my prayers. He showed me that when I commit to Him and His plan, He will provide and equip.

As we arrived at Fort Rucker, dear friends of ours already stationed there graciously invited us to live with them until on-post housing was available. We lived with them for ten days. My friend Donna was a wonderful cook and extremely organized. In those ten short days I began to learn some things that I knew would help me in my new role. I left her home with some new recipes and ideas for establishing our new home.

God began to show me the truth in the saying that "Army wives are special." Amazingly we had wonderful military families surrounding us. They welcomed our family with home-cooked meals and watched our only child Elizabeth for us as we moved in. The Lord was showing His provision and love for me through these military spouses. I was also witnessing, firsthand, why army wives are special. I prayed for help and these women were a big part of God's answer.

Fortunately God gave me a very patient husband with a sense of humor. Every morning I would ask my husband, an excellent cook, his advice on how to prepare dinner. He would come home after work with a smile on his face in curious anticipation of the surprise I had prepared for him. He was always patient. One evening the peppered flank steak was so spicy that our Labrador wouldn't even eat it! My husband endured many challenging dinners, but he maintained a sense of humor and continued to encourage me.

God was transforming my heart during this time of my life as I was learning the tasks necessary to manage our home. He was teaching me about humility as I relied on my husband and my friends for advice and help in being the "keeper of my home" (Titus 2). I also learned to ask God daily for the wisdom to be a good mother. In Proverbs 3:34, God promises to give grace to the humble. As those were all weak areas of my life that I could not conquer in my own strength, I certainly was in a place of humility. I learned to walk in God's grace daily and memorized 2 Corinthians 12:9, "My grace is sufficient for you, for My strength is made perfect in weakness." God was showing me that He was going to get the glory from my life because I was so weak and in need of His help!

As I continued to pray for God's help, He always answered, whether it was practically, through my husband and friends, or directly from His heart. I would read in His word, and He would give me exactly what I needed to hear for that moment or day. "The Lord is my strength and shield, my heart trusted in Him and I am helped," Psalm 28:7, was one of those verses I needed to hear. At Fort Rucker I realized what a special job it was to take care of our young family and support my soldier. It was God's plan to allow me to need Him so desperately in the everyday tasks of keeping our home. For the first time in my life, I was learning to rely on Him for the smallest of things.

I had been at home full-time for eight months when my husband graduated as the distinguished honor graduate of the Aviation Officer Career Course. I was so proud of him. It occurred to me that day that my heart to support him during the course had helped him "be all he could be." It was the first time in our marriage that I had worked hard to complete my husband, helping him to achieve his goals.

God showed me the commitment I had to make to support my soldier. There were volunteer functions, fund raisers, and Family Readiness Group meetings. The FRG leaders amazed me with all they did without being paid. Wives surrounded me, both those who had careers outside of the home and those whose careers were full-time stay-at-home wives and mothers just like me. All of us had the same choice to make. Were we going to decide to accept with our whole heart the commitment of this military lifestyle?

My husband continued to speak words of encouragement

and praise over me. These words replaced the awards and ribbons the Army would have given me for a job well done. His words brought life to me in the midst of my failures. My husband was awarding me daily for the sacrifice I had made to lay down my career in support of his. I began to see this lifestyle quite differently. My identity was no longer in the Army but instead in God and what He had for me each day as I invested in my husband and our family.

As we finished our tour at Fort Rucker, my husband received a call to try out for the 160th Special Operations Aviation Regiment. While I knew little about the organization, I encouraged my soldier to do his best, telling him I would follow him wherever he went. Rich returned with news that the evaluation within the unit went very well and we would be moving to Fort Campbell to join the ranks of the "Nightstalkers."

We spent the next five years with the 160th. God took me there to teach me what the word "commitment" really meant. He exposed me to some of the best military spouses I had ever met. They taught and encouraged me as I led a company-level Family Readiness Group twice during our tour. The company's families looked to me as their leader, mentor, and friend. It took a lot of time to get to know these special families, but it was worth every minute. The unit's mission was so demanding it bound us together in support of one another. "Army Wives are Special," rang true in my life. Sometimes the commitment to support our husbands was very painful and difficult. Yet, as we experienced constant separations, often unexpected, we were there for each other. With kindred spirits, we befriended one another, celebrated life together and lived through times of unknown missions, the next possible communication, as well as times of sorrow and tragedy with the loss of life. We were wives of warriors who were committed to support the call placed on their lives to protect and defend our nation.

In February 2003, my husband and I attended the Pre-Command Course at Fort Leavenworth, Kansas, and were blessed to hear at that time, from the top military leaders in our Army. The Army chief of staff, General Eric Shinseki, and his wife spoke to us. They emphasized that a military couple is a team. I left encouraged by the difference I do make in my role as a supportive spouse alongside my husband. I realized it also included our children who are serving our nation as we live out this unique and often difficult lifestyle.

Sergeant Major of the Army Jack Tilley also spoke to us. He pointed out the importance of our job to love God, love our families, and love the Army family we have the privilege to serve with as we strive for the same purpose. He said we are all soldiers. Having served in the Army, I can say a soldier's life is not easy, but supporting my soldier in my role as a military spouse for more than twenty years has truly been one of the most challenging things I have ever done! Sergeant Major Tilley's words reminded me that even in the difficult times, my job as a military spouse is important and it does make a difference.

I have always been amazed by the life of Martha Washington. She was a great example of a woman embracing her commitment to her military man in the early days of American history. Her commitment to her soldier and what he was doing illustrates the profound impact she made on the future of our nation. She left the comforts of Mt. Vernon to live at Valley Forge during the winter of 1777-1778. Using that time as an opportunity to support her husband, she did many things to care for his men in a practical way. One example is she chose to knit socks for his soldiers. This may seem very small, but accounts from history tell us most of Washington's men marched to Valley Forge in the beginning of the winter with no boots or shoes. She also spoke words of encouragement to her soldier as well as his men.

I believe Martha's willingness to support her soldier and make the commitment to endure the lifestyle, no matter the cost, had a tremendous impact on the outcome of that long winter at Valley Forge. She supported her soldier, the commander of the entire army. I have learned it is a privilege to do the same for my soldier!

CHAPTER 3
SEPARATION AND LONELINESS

Be strong and courageous; do not be afraid, for
the Lord your God is with you wherever you go.
Joshua 1:9
Be of good courage, and He shall strengthen
your heart, all you who hope in the Lord.
Psalms 31:24

Have you ever felt lost, hopeless, unsure, and afraid? Have
you ever been suddenly lost? Once when I was four years old,
I was separated from my dad. I was in unfamiliar surroundings,
complete with strangers. It was a terrible feeling. Who could I
trust for help? My dad and I were on a very crowded elevator
and all I remember is when the door opened my dad stepped
out. Before I could get around the people the door closed! I was
separated from the one who was my source of comfort and
protection in such a big, unusual place. Even though I was
surrounded by people, I felt all alone. I rode the elevator
through a number of different floors before the door opened and

I saw my dad standing there. I ran into his arms and would not let go. The time I spent riding on that elevator alone seemed like an eternity.

The military lifestyle requires separation from the people, places and things we know and love. At times we feel lost, with feelings of loneliness as our constant companion. The situations of separation may be different but the feelings are very much the same: loneliness, hopelessness, uncertainty, and fear. I remember our first tour in the military, as well as I do our sixth assignment, and with each situation the initial feelings were the same.

My husband has told me many times of his own feelings of loneliness. It changed my perspective to know my soldier has experienced times of loneliness too; especially during a deployment. It has prevented me from blaming my husband in the midst of a difficult situation and to understand that he, as well as the girls and I, were struggling with the same feelings of loneliness. This has enabled me to support him in each new unit and has allowed us to work through these emotions together.

The shock of military life is often toughest on new service members and their families. I remember vividly my own feelings of loneliness as a cadet in Airborne School and then again as a new second lieutenant at my first duty assignment at Fort Rucker, Alabama. In both instances, I was experiencing culture shock from leaving my home in Wisconsin, to live in a place where everything seemed foreign to me.

A young spouse, brand new to the military lifestyle told me before she made any friends she put a lot of pressure on her husband to entertain her after arriving home from work. She emphasized her feelings to want to get out of the house because she had been alone all day with their infant son. She spoke of her husband's compassion for her situation, but he communicated to her that he also was trying to fit into his new unit. It was then they both realized they had to do something. She shared with me Proverbs 18:24, which says, "A man who has friends must himself be friendly." It became the solution to their problem as it motivated them to take the first step, get involved in their community, their new unit and make some new friends.

In today's Army, young couples are coming into the military and facing immediate deployments to Iraq and Afghanistan. I personally know many such couples from Fort Bragg, North Carolina. Some are newly married, now living in the Fort Bragg area. They were given only a few months together in the area before being separated due to scheduled deployments to the war zone. These women personally told me of their feelings of loneliness and of how hard it was to find a "life" in a new place, without their husbands. Some of these women, just like me, battled feelings to want to return back home, to what they knew and to what seemed safe and secure. For others it was the desire to return to the place of their previous assignment. Both desires stemmed from the same emotion of feeling all alone.

My journey of being married to my soldier has at times overwhelmed me with feelings of loneliness. One such story began when my husband received orders in March of 1993. We had been in the military for eight years; this was to be our fourth move. I felt certain this would be our best move, as I considered myself a seasoned military spouse. I was surprised when I began to experience feelings of isolation and loneliness. I kept telling myself to snap out of it, but with each day it became more unbearable. We were newly assigned to the 160th Special Aviation Regiment at Fort Campbell, Kentucky. We had been in the area a few weeks, living in the guest house, as my husband in-processed. This experience was an event in itself. Before checking into the guest house, I had grand plans of continuing to educate our kindergartner. I failed to realize how difficult this would be in a cramped, crowded room, with a two-and-a-half- and a one-year-old underfoot. Not only that, but I was also experiencing severe morning sickness. I really was trying to make the most of our situation but there was nowhere to go. We had just left the Sunshine Belt of the south, only to be shocked by the cold and dreary days in the Midwest. The temperature barely rose above forty degrees. We would go out to play but wouldn't last long. My husband would return in the afternoon so we could go house hunting. We were thrilled to be out of our tiny living space, but driving around, trying to find the perfect house with three small children climbing in and out of a minivan wasn't my idea of fun. Once we finally found the perfect house, I anxiously awaited moving in. I reminded myself I only had to endure the guest house a few more days and then life would certainly be "all better" again.

We finally moved into our new home off post. We received our household goods the very next day and we spent the weekend unpacking as much as we could before my husband began his initial phase of training called Green Platoon. I was totally unprepared for the difficult schedule we would all have to endure for the next ten weeks. Life, in fact, did not get better but worse. Most of my husband's training would occur at night. He came home long enough to eat, shower and sleep. He would arrive home in the wee hours of the morning and then sleep until noon. He would grab a shower and some lunch and then head back out the door with very little time for any of us. It was a difficult schedule for the family because we had three young daughters who were full of life and energy. It was cold outside so we spent a lot of time playing in the garage so we would not disturb Dad's sleep.

My feelings of loneliness were overwhelming because my husband had no time for me. I did my best to try and stay positive. As our second daughter Hannah's birthday arrived I tried to make it as normal as possible. I wanted to include her daddy in the celebration so I made her wait to open her presents until he got up. He tried to participate but the truth was he was consumed by the stresses of his training and the crazy schedule. He gave her a hug and then left for another long day. As a young military spouse it was hard to understand it wasn't his choice, but the demand of the training he was involved in. As a family, we felt very isolated because we were not yet a part of the unit. There would be no "welcome" calls until he successfully graduated from the course. This was not something we were used to. Again I tried to be a supportive army wife and wait patiently for my husband to successfully graduate from the course so I could finally receive an initial welcome and meet some new friends within the family readiness group.

It was a very long ten weeks. Our children were small and the first six weeks the weather was cold, which made it difficult to meet our neighbors. We had not found a church home yet, and locating the local home-school group was harder than I thought. Because we had not met anyone, the girls and I felt quite alone. The feeling was extreme. I felt totally isolated. It was during this time, and the months that followed, in a unit where my husband was constantly deployed that God began a new work in my heart. In those initial ten weeks, with three small children and no other adult to talk to, I found myself spending more and more time talking to God. He never audibly spoke back, but I began to have a sense of comfort and peace.

Even if I couldn't tell someone who understood how lonely I felt, I could tell God and I knew He understood. His word promised me that He was near to all who called upon Him (Psalms 145:18). I was learning to cast all my cares upon God, knowing He cared for me and our girls, and that He knew my circumstance (1 Peter 5:7).

It was during this time in my life I found the verses in Psalm 73:25-26, 28. The words spoke straight to my heart. They said exactly what I was learning. "Whom have I in heaven but You? And there is none upon earth that I desire besides you." My flesh and my heart will fail; but God was becoming the strength of my heart and my portion forever. Verse 28 confirmed what I was feeling. It was good for me to draw near to God, and to put my trust in Him, so I could tell of His works. I recognized that God was doing a work in me even though it was very painful. It was as if God took my husband out of my life on purpose to show me He was always there for me. Early in our marriage Rich and I committed to put time aside each night to talk even as our children came along. With his current training schedule he barely had enough time to get any sleep, much less have time to talk to me. He wasn't able to be my confidant and friend during those long weeks of training. I thought I was doing my part in supporting my soldier, but he had no time to support and care for me.

Being an avid reader was a tremendous help during this time as I finished historical novels on previous military spouses that I truly came to admire. Women who had lived through what I was experiencing in those first months at Fort Campbell built a bridge in my heart from loneliness to hope. I realized my only hope was in a sovereign God who had chosen this assignment for our family as well as any deployments we would face in the future. In moments of heavy-heartedness, I would remind myself I was not alone because God promised to always be with me (Joshua 1:9). It was through these times of loneliness and isolation, God became my best friend. I realized that He had to be enough. As I began to speak to Him throughout my day, I felt His presence in a new way. I realized that I didn't have to wait until Sunday morning where I would be surrounded by a church full of people. God was willing and waiting to meet with me all by myself, anytime, anywhere.

Since that time, I have often shared the testimony of how God answered my prayers for peace and a sense of contentment for the new place He had decided we were to call home.

God wanted me to remember how He helped me through these difficult times. I learned through my experience what mattered most to God was what I decided to do with my feelings of loneliness and isolation. Was I going to allow my circumstances to cripple me or would I choose to be teachable and grow through them?

Psalm 25:4-5 says, "Show me your ways, O Lord; teach me your paths. Lead me in your truth and teach me, for you are the God of my salvation; on you I wait all the day." Waiting for me is a difficult task. I am a woman. I want to know all the details and I want to have my say in how the details will play out in my life and that of my family. God is, however, teaching me to wait, especially in times of trial. I asked God to help me to always be willing to learn. The challenge is waiting patiently and allowing God to establish our family's steps in each new place. God encouraged me through Psalm 40:1-2, "I waited patiently for the Lord; and He inclined to me, and heard my cry. He also brought me up out of a horrible pit, out of the miry clay, and set my feet upon a rock, and established my steps."

When I was so lonely, I felt like I was surrounded by four tall walls, without a way to escape. I felt trapped in a situation that I could not change. I could not go to my husband's commanding officer demanding that he change my husband's work schedule because I needed him. Instead, I cried out to God, asking Him to show me what He was trying to teach me.

I learned two very important lessons from that extreme time of loneliness. The first: God is faithful to meet me wherever I am. Whether my faith is as solid as a rock, or if my faith is as sinking sand, He still loves me. He proved to me as I drew near to Him, that He would draw near to me (James 4:8). It was a priceless lesson. Secondly, I learned that wherever I was, no matter my circumstance, I could make a difference. I felt the Lord establish my steps and put in me, through this difficult time, a passion to reach out and encourage other military spouses in a similar situation. It began in the unit's Family Readiness Group, whether the ladies participated or not. I took the time to call them, introduce myself and give them my phone number. I also purposed to meet the new families moving into our neighborhood. Some families became dear friends, others just acquaintances, but each one knew where we lived and that they could call if they needed us. My goal was to make sure these ladies understood that someone recognized they were new and cared about them. I did not want them to have the same kind of struggle I had experienced as the new family on the block. We continued to live the next five and one-half years at Fort Campbell, Kentucky, assigned to the same special operations aviation unit. We faced countless numbers of deployments that included new moments of loneliness. The difference was that I now held the key that opened the door to my lonely heart. I knew that as I reached out to others, my own feelings of loneliness would fade away.

It has been over fifteen years since my first lesson of God's presence and faithfulness during my times of loneliness and separation. I still must prepare my heart for each move and deployment. I begin by reading and meditating on Psalm 27:13-14, which says, "I would have lost heart, unless I had believed that I would see the goodness of the Lord in the land of the living. Wait on the Lord; be of good courage, and He shall strengthen your heart; wait, I say, on the Lord!" As a military spouse, I now understand there is a requirement on my life to learn to wait. God does not want me to lose heart in my challenging situations, but to trust in Him for the outcome.

A young spouse, new to the military, expresses it best. Upon arriving at their first duty station, she said her feelings of loneliness were overwhelming. She began to wonder, "Did I make the right decision of marrying into the military? I love my husband but I had no idea what it would feel like to leave my home and move half way across the country." As this young spouse was working through her trial of loneliness, she discovered the verses in 2 Corinthians 1, which told her that God was the God of all comfort, who comforts us in our trials. It completely changed her outlook on her situation. She realized the truth that God knew exactly how she was feeling and that one day God would use her to comfort someone just as He had comforted her.

The outcome of her difficult time of loneliness taught her a very important life lesson. As she allowed God into her situation He was able to comfort her. In turn, He wanted her to use her testimony to comfort and encourage others.

As a military spouse one of the most important things God has taught me is that I must choose not to dwell on my difficult situation. I cannot change the extremely long working hours required of my soldier or whether or not he will be deployed. The only thing I can change is my attitude. Just as a baby must be brave enough to take his or her first step, I must choose to take the first step of faith to make my situation better. The story of Mary in Luke 10 illustrates it best. She demonstrated her faith and clung to her hope as she sat at Jesus' feet. In spite of all that was going on around her she chose the one thing that was most needed and could not be taken from her.

I believe our daily dependence on God for our inner joy,

peace and strength is what impacts our attitude the most, but how do we help ourselves practically? The following is a quote from a very experienced military spouse.

"Like you, I find things that have helped sustain me in the long separations that we face as military spouses. One of the things I've always done is have had something in my life that was somewhat unrelated to the military, such as my job, which gave me a different group of individuals to get to know and enjoy, and something else to learn. And, definitely like you, I have used my running/working out to maintain my stress!"

The words of this seasoned military spouse highlight the importance of taking care of our physical mind and body as we face the challenges of this lifestyle.

As I remember my own past experiences of loneliness and separation it continues to motivate me to reach out and make a difference in the lives of the women and families God puts in my path.

Through my trials God has given me a passion to encourage and support other military spouses through the challenges we each encounter in this lifestyle. I believe with the title "Military Spouse" comes the unique ability to positively impact our nation. Through our words of encouragement and acts of support to our warriors as well as to one another, we each are doing our part to retain a national asset, "The Military Family." It is important to understand, the military doesn't just recruit a soldier, sailor, airman, or marine; it must recruit the whole family. I know I have a vital part in completing that mission. As I rely on the strength of the Lord He enables me to be a strong army wife who in turn helps sustain a strong soldier!

CHAPTER 4
MAKING THE MOST OF EVERY OPPORTUNITY

"You are the light of the world. A city that is set
on a hill cannot be hidden."
Matthew 5:14
"Through love serve one another."
Galatians 5:13

Have you ever considered your role as a military spouse or as a military family one that would require a vision? Proverbs 29:18 says, "Where there is no vision, the people perish." Over the years our family vision has changed as our family has matured, but one of the enduring aspects has been the desire to "make the most of every opportunity."

Until I resigned my commission in the U.S. Army, we had no family vision. The Army's needs came first, at the cost of our baby girl. Her schedule was set by our long days of work. A normal day for me was to rise by 4:45AM to feed and dress Elizabeth and then drive her to the sitter. On a good day, I would pick her up at 6:30 PM, but many times it was even later. Life was chaotic and stressful. After resigning from the Army my new job title became "full-time wife and mother." Our lifestyle completely changed from one filled with the stresses and challenges of a dual military family to one filled with stability and peacefulness. I believe this change is what brought us to a place where God could reveal His true plan for our lives.

During this time, we were on our second tour at Fort Rucker, but this time we were married. As a family, we were committed to working with youth at the local Methodist Church we were attending. We were excited about the difference we were making. My husband began wrestling with the idea of resigning and becoming a youth pastor. After much prayer, he put in his resignation packet. We were sure that his resignation would be approved as it was during a draw down and the military was paying people to get out. We began making plans to move to Lexington, Kentucky, as Rich had been accepted to Asbury Seminary. Life was going along smoothly. Rich was finishing his advanced course, and he felt it would be an easy transition from school into the civilian sector of life. He would not be leaving a unit, or creating a shortfall and leaving the army mission in jeopardy.

As my husband's resignation paperwork passed through the chain of command for approval, he was summoned to speak with both the brigade and post commanders. Neither one could understand why my husband wanted to get out of the military. He had just graduated as the Distinguished Honor Graduate from the Aviation Advanced Course. Rich tried to explain his desire to make a difference as a youth pastor. The post commander's response to my husband's desire to resign had a profound impact on our family. First, he denied my husband's resignation and then he said, "Your mission field is right here. You can make a positive difference in the United States Army!"

I was shocked when Rich came home with this piece of news, but he told me not to worry because he felt totally at peace and that the general's advice was the best he had ever received. God used the wise council of that general officer to change my husband's vision regarding his army career, as well as giving us a real vision for our family.

As we waited for orders for our next assignment, we began to ask God to show us ways to make a difference. As it turned out, Rich was chosen to stay at Fort Rucker as a TAC officer in the Aviation Training Brigade. His job was to train new aviators for eight weeks, as they finished the flight phase of training and were now transitioning to their first unit assignments. Rich felt it was a great place to impact young leaders in our Army.

Prior to my getting out of the service, my husband had been a company commander in the 9ᵗʰ Aviation Brigade at Fort Lewis. Along with his command came my role as the Family Readiness Group Leader. It was a difficult position for me. As much as I wanted to do a good job, I merely survived due to my own responsibilities as a battalion adjutant, aviator, wife, and mother! Betty Crocker became my hero, as her boxed desserts were all I had time to make for any Family Readiness event. It was also very difficult to spend quality time getting to know the ladies and their families within the unit.

Now, as Rich was assigned to train and mentor young soldiers at Fort Rucker, I felt God was giving me a second chance to make a difference in the lives of their young wives. For the first time as a couple, we embraced my husband's position and considered it a wonderful opportunity to invest our lives through serving and encouraging these young military couples and their families. Many of these couples became very dear to us and have continued to be lifelong friends. We are very grateful for our time at Fort Rucker and how God used Rich's plan to resign as the catalyst to discover how to look at this military lifestyle as one of opportunity. God eventually gave my husband the verse from Matthew 5:16. It says, "Let your light so shine before men, that they may see your good works and glorify your Father in heaven."

Our family vision became one of being involved, reaching out, caring for and serving others. We wanted our lives to demonstrate the love of God.

At this time, our children were extremely young. So our "good works" were somewhat limited. Outreach was done from our home. We often invited young couples over for snacks as I still was not a very good cook, but I resolved in my heart it wasn't about how delicious a dinner I could serve as much as it was about getting to know these new military families. With a dear friend's help, I volunteered to host many FRG (Family Readiness Group) events. I got involved with the Fort Rucker community through the post chapel, participating in both Moms of Preschoolers and Protestant Woman of the Chapel. Much of my service was done while volunteering in childcare. I was a young mother with small children so I felt the best place to make a difference was right where the Lord had me in my life. What I gained by learning to serve others by watching their small children was far more than what I gave. I grew a lot as I poured my life into others' children.

As we moved on to Fort Campbell, Kentucky, our girls were six, almost three and eighteen months. I took them with me to every volunteer event that allowed children. I knew they would learn to serve by watching my example. They began by watching but ended up having many hands-on experiences to serve as well, during our five years at Fort Campbell.

In a previous chapter, I discussed how the separation from the people we love and the familiarity of the places we know causes feelings of loneliness. God used such a time in my own life to teach me to make the most of my situation by reaching out to others. We had just moved into our new neighborhood. We didn't wait for our neighbors to come to us, we went to them. Our girls and I filled our wagon with homemade goodies and went door to door, introducing ourselves. Our girls loved their part in it. They claimed ownership of what they had helped to make. They even fought over who would carry the "goody" up to each door. In many cases, the initial meetings turned into more opportunities to spend time with our neighbors. Special friendships were formed and all of us were blessed by it.

I often remind myself of the wonderful friendships our family would have missed, had we not taken the opportunity to reach out to our neighbors. It has become a Juergens family tradition to meet our neighbors as quickly as possible at each new place. We consider this to be one of the best examples of making the most of every opportunity (Colossians 4:2).

It was also during this time that I committed in my heart to pray for more opportunities as I chose to make the most of our new assignment and those that were in our future. As God knew my thoughts, I believe He put me to the test. My husband had just relinquished his company command of eighteen months. I was looking forward to a slower-paced life with less responsibility, as my role as the Family Readiness Group leader also came to a close. God definitely had something else in mind.

A few weeks later, I was asked by the single captain preparing to command the headquarters company if I would accept the position of his Family Readiness Group leader. My initial thought was, "No way, I can't handle another leadership position!" Then I remembered the commitment I had made to make the most of every opportunity. There were many qualified ladies to do the job but I had been the first woman he asked to take the position. I presented the situation to our family, and those who understood agreed it must be where God needed me the most. I realized I had no other choice but to say yes.

It turned out to be a wonderful year. It was filled with new friendships and opportunities to help and encourage other army families just like us. As a home-school family I was able to include into our daily schedule the times we were needed to help serve others outside our home. Our girls were getting older so the year was a first to truly help and not just be dragged along. As they served that year they quickly learned what the term "Army Family" really meant. We did not just help with special events; we helped take care of each other as most of us were separated from our extended families. Over the years, within each Family Readiness Group, our daughters have had numerous opportunities to look not to their own interests but the interests of other (Philippians 2:4). Bake sales, lunch sales, and you-name-it fundraisers…they were there! They have been there for many different occasions, decorating and cleaning up for both company and battalion functions. They have stuffed many a goody bag going to deployed soldiers overseas. Once, they even spent the day with me, without complaining as I tried to calm and comfort a spouse who had boarded herself inside her home. She was a brand-new army wife. Fear had gotten the best of her as her husband was deployed for the very first time. I even had one of my daughters go with me to serve as needed as I helped a young wife who was experiencing a miscarriage.

She needed emotional support and physical help because her soldier was gone. These times were priceless in our daughters' lives as they formed in their hearts a desire to serve.

A wonderful example of this happened with our year spent at Fort Leavenworth, Kansas. We knew it would be a great year as Rich would be a student at the Command and General Staff College. The requirement to attend the school meant he would be home for eleven straight months! The girls and I were thrilled. We were excited to look for opportunities to reach out and serve as a whole family.

The post chapel was looking for families willing to host and teach neighborhood Bible studies. My husband immediately volunteered. It was exciting to see the enthusiasm in our girls as Wednesday night Bible study approached each week. They didn't care that poached eggs became the norm for dinner because it was quick and easy. They couldn't wait to have ten more children invade our home for games, music, and crafts. Our oldest daughter was now in the fifth grade with four younger sisters. As a born leader, she embraced the opportunity to invest in the younger children who came to our home each week.

My husband and I considered it a privilege to serve and get to know our neighbors in this way. These relationships grew into deep friendships. A family in our church offered their oldest daughter's help to assist me with all the children. It was a huge answer to prayer. I definitely had my concerns as I thought about being responsible for ten extra children each week. This special young lady, named Corrie, along with the rest of her family are some of our dearest friends to this day. We often talk about those sweet memories from our weekly get-togethers and what we would have missed if we had not been willing to open our hearts and home. As a family we have found that opportunities present themselves as we make ourselves available.

Our family vision of making the most of every opportunity was growing as our oldest daughters were embracing it for themselves.

As Rich and I continued to be involved with each unit and the Family Readiness Group, our girls were looking for ways they could volunteer to make a difference. As our oldest turned twelve she began volunteering to help young moms in our neighborhood. She set a tremendous example for the rest of our older girls as they became babysitting age. Elizabeth also set the example to teach beginner piano, at a reduced rate. Her heart was to allow parents an inexpensive way to find out if their children really wanted to play the piano. Our next four daughters have followed in her shoes by continuing to do the same in each new neighborhood. Our daughters' willingness to be available has allowed them to serve others and earn a little money, as well as some work experience. Ultimately, it has allowed us to meet and impact many new families.

Wonderful opportunities have presented themselves as our

daughters have participated in sports and other extracurricular activities. How we have chosen to make the most of these activities is by encouraging our children to use their talents as a way to reach out and bless others.

Our oldest daughter has used her talent and love for sports as a way to do just that. At the age of sixteen, she volunteered to coach the youth services 10-12 year-old soccer team, taking them to a playoff tournament in Seoul, South Korea. She also volunteered to run and coach a youth basketball clinic at Camp Humphreys, South Korea.

Our middle daughters have a love for children as well. Over the last four years they have volunteered through youth services to help younger children in the homework lab. They have also volunteered in the post chapel and at our local church for vacation Bible school. Our third daughter, at fourteen, volunteered to be a part of a mission trip to Costa Rica. Each one of these events has fueled the desire in our daughters' hearts to continue to look for ways to serve and reach out. Our oldest daughter Elizabeth, now twenty, shares her testimony:

"When I was growing up, my parents instilled in me the importance of making the most of every opportunity. During my sophomore and junior year of high school, I played varsity basketball at Osan American High School, South Korea. Playing basketball was my passion but I used it as a way to make a difference in the lives of my teammates and my coach. I'm currently a full-time college student, and working part-time. I have taken many opportunities in class and at work to reach out to others. I continue each day to pray for ways to make the most of every opportunity. It truly is a part of who I am."

With each new duty assignment, our family has tried to use our life experiences to help others. We began our home-schooling journey when our oldest turned five. Over the last fifteen years, we have belonged to a home-schooling group. Whether through our church or within the local community, our goal has been to be involved and to make a difference. Initially, as we were the rookies, Rich and I volunteered our talents in support of the group. We helped organize and lead many gym days. We loved being there to encourage the children as their confidence grew in their physical abilities. As a college graduate, I took the steps to become a certified standardized test administrator. I have been able to use this as a way to serve others as a volunteer to test their children.

Once we hit the ten-year mark as home educators, we began to seek out ways to mentor new home-schooling families.

As for our family and the examples I have given, it's not the fact that any of us are overly talented, but rather we are willing and committed to making a positive difference wherever we go! I certainly don't want to portray the image that our family is always in the midst of some life-changing event. In fact, more of our time is spent just trying to make a difference in the everyday kind of stuff. The everyday stuff starts in our home. Stuff like speaking words of encouragement, being a good listener, lending a helping hand, being faithful in chores or even the simplest smile of kindness toward one another; all of which can totally change someone's day.

Following the simple scripture in I Corinthians 16:14 which says, "Let all that you do be done in love," along with my grandma's favorite, "Do unto others as your want them to do to you" (Matthew 7:12), makes doing the simple, everyday stuff easy. My grandma often reminded me of her favorite verse. It has impacted my daily actions throughout my life, as well as becoming a favorite verse in our own home as we have taught our girls to make the most of every opportunity. We continue to remind them that what may seem to be insignificant often has the biggest influence on someone's life.

Let me share just one example from my own life. It was a typical trip to the extremely busy post office. As always, there was a long line and it wasn't moving very quickly. As soon as I walked through the door I could feel the tension in the room. People were beginning to complain. In the midst of this, I took the opportunity to spark up a conversation with the two people on either side of me. One woman was also a military spouse. I don't remember exactly what I said and after leaving the post office, I never gave it another thought. A few months later as I was being introduced as one of the new mentors at the local MOPS (mothers of preschoolers) meeting, a woman stood up and said, "I know you. You were the woman who encouraged me and changed the whole mood in the post office." No one was more shocked than me. Who could imagine meeting the same stranger twice in the city the size of Fayetteville, North Carolina. I felt as if God was whispering in my ear, "The smallest things do make a difference to someone, especially to me!"

We are a family on the lookout. Before we leave our home, whether just to run errands or to go on a long family vacation, we ask God to give us eyes to see opportunities that would make a difference in someone's life. Our motivation is driven by our love for God (Matthew 22:37), and by His heart that we love one another (Galatians 5:13). At our house, that means looking for ways to love people, by reaching out, caring for, and serving them. Our hope is that ultimately our actions will bring glory to God (1 Corinthians 10:31).

God has touched our lives in special ways and built our faith because of our passion to follow the family vision. The following are just a few amazing examples.

One of our favorites happened many years ago. The girls and I were on a road trip from Kentucky to Wisconsin to visit my mom. Our family travels with a cooler full of food and uses rest stops as the destination for long breaks, eating, and play. On this particular day, the girls and I had just piled out of the van. While walking our dogs, we spotted another family on the playground. We went over with the family vision in mind. I reminded our little girls to be friendly, take turns and have fun! It turned out to be another home-schooling family from

Arkansas on their way to New Jersey. My new acquaintance Theresa and I were traveling without our husbands so, as women do, we took advantage of the time to talk and get to know more about one another. We also agreed it was great our children were playing well together so they would be worn out by the time they got back into our vans. We found we had much in common, the obvious common thread being the size of our families. We had four little girls under the age of seven and my new friend Theresa had five boys of similar age. We spent over an hour encouraging one another as mothers of large families, moms traveling with young children, and as home educators. We were all sad at our need to get back on the road. We said our goodbyes, prayed for each other's safety, and left. As we continued on our way, the girls and I marveled at God's love for us to allow us to meet such a neat family at a rest stop!

The following year our whole family was once again making the trip from Kentucky to Wisconsin to visit Grandma. We planned to stop at the same rest stop, as it had become a favorite! As we began walking to the picnic area, I couldn't believe what I saw. I grabbed my husband's arm and said, "You will never believe this but that is the same family we met here last year!" He said, "No way!" As we approached the playground, Theresa and I made eye contact. Neither of us could believe it! We waited a moment to speak. Then we both began to speak at once. We began to laugh and then realized our children were already playing as if they were best friends. The only difference was that we were blessed this time to be traveling with our husbands.

Once again, we spent a long time at the rest stop, encouraging one another and building each other up (1 Thessalonians 5:11). When we saw each other the second time, it was as if we had been lifelong friends. We knew it was totally by God's hand we met for a second time. This time before saying goodbye, we exchanged addresses and promised to stay in touch.

Over the years, we have been extremely blessed by the annual Christmas letters and updated family pictures we have shared. To this day, we continue to share this unbelievable story with others. It all began because the girls and I purposed to make the most of an opportunity by just being friendly.

Our family agrees that one of the absolute best opportunities we have had as a military family is traveling: seeing new places, and of course meeting new people. Oftentimes this happens as we travel between each duty station and back home to spend time with family and friends.

My second amazing example happened as we were traveling home from visiting family in Maryland. We had just spent the night in South Carolina and we were enjoying our continental breakfast, compliments of the hotel. Due to the size of our family, we were a spectacle. Within a few minutes my husband and I were having an intriguing conversation with an older couple beside us. They suspected my husband was in the military. It was tough to hide his haircut! We found out the gentleman was a WWII veteran, who also loved his country and God. He thanked my husband for his service to our nation and then turned his eyes to the girls and me and thanked us for our sacrifice as well. He then proceeded to share some of his war stories. Again, we spent much longer than we had planned for breakfast. We considered it a privilege to get to know this couple who had lived the life we were living. They were a true encouragement to us that day. We exchanged e-mail addresses and phone numbers. Over the years, Mr. France has been a continued support to our family by his prayers, especially for my husband, and through his phone calls of encouragement. It never fails. Mr. France always calls to check on us when Rich is deployed. Each time I hear his voice it reminds me of how much God loves me. His calls faithfully come when I am discouraged. God has used Mr. France to speak words of hope into my life exactly when I have needed it.

God has blessed us over the years with the friendship of this faithful couple. We believe it happened because we were willing to make the most of the opportunity when we first met.

Another example is centered on the life of a young soldier, who became very dear to our family. We invested in this young man's life over the period of a year, as we were stationed together at Camp Humphreys, South Korea. He left Korea a year ahead of us on his way to the 101st Airborne Division at Fort Campbell, Kentucky. Since we had lived in the Fort

Campbell area for over five years, we gave him the name of the church we had attended. We lost contact for a few years but recently, through a mutual dear friend, we were able to get his phone number and give him a call. He couldn't believe it when I identified myself over the phone. He told me he was trying to find a way to reach us as he had wonderful news. He was getting married! The amazing part of his news was the fact that he was marrying the oldest daughter of one of our closest family friends from Fort Campbell. He had no idea we knew his fiancée until he showed her a picture of our family. He told me he had wanted his fiancée to see the family that had impacted his life in so many ways, especially in the area of marriage. Only God could plan such a divine meeting. The coolest part for us was hearing this young man's testimony of the positive difference we had made in his life.

It was confirmation to our whole family. Our willingness to be involved in other people's lives truly makes a difference.

My husband and I believe being a military family is the call God has placed on our lives. We also believe we have been given a specific vision on how we are to live out our call. We teach our children the heart of the family vision to touch lives and make a positive difference. We purpose to incorporate the vision into our daily lives. It is what motivates our every action and decision. Our oldest daughters are totally sold out to God and for the vision He gave our family so many years ago but we continue to encourage our younger girls ages three, six, nine, and eleven to look for opportunities as well. I saw they were getting the vision just recently as we were out eating a snack at Costco. Our youngest daughter, Olivia, started waving and smiling at an elderly lady sitting at the table across from us. This initiated a conversation that lasted for nearly an hour. We found out she was seventy-six years old, had four grown children, loved greyhound dogs and knew she couldn't do anything without God's help. As we were preparing to leave Costco our eleven-year-old, Grace, voluntarily walked over to clear her table and say goodbye. The woman tried to pay Grace. Grace refused the money but insisted she allow each girl to give her a goodbye hug. This sweet lady was deeply touched by their acts of kindness but not as deeply as I was to watch our youngest daughters extend the love of God to a complete stranger without my prodding them. It was as if I were watching the family vision being played out except this time I had no big part in it.

One last story began one Sunday morning while at church. Our senior pastor made an announcement that a number of foreign exchange students still needed homes by the end of the week or else they would not have the chance to come to the U.S. I immediately thought, "What is one more girl in our house?" This would be yet another opportunity to love and invest in someone else. I also thought it would be a life-changing experience for our children. On the way home, I asked our girls what they thought about the idea. Everyone was excited. My husband was deployed, so I sent an e-mail with a hope he would respond quickly. He called that very night and said, "Go for it!" First thing Monday morning, I called the agency to volunteer to host a female student from South Korea.

Under normal circumstance, a host family is required to familiarize themselves with the culture of the country prior to their student's arrival. With such little notice, we were confident of our ability to relate to a Korean student as we had spent two years at Camp Humphreys, South Korea. Eleven days later, the girls and I were picking up our foreign exchange student, Hyo-Jin Lee, at the airport. Prior to coming to the States, Hyo-Jin had been faxed a description of our family. A few days before she arrived, we received a letter she had written many months prior for her potential host family. In it she described herself as quiet but happy, an only child, and the daughter of a pastor. The amazing bit of information was the fact that she was from the exact area where we had lived for our two years in her country. As a family, we had spent a great deal of time in her hometown, hanging out with two Korean couples who became dear friends. We couldn't wait to tell her. Once she knew, Hyo-Jin immediately told her parents in Korea. Her parents and our dear friends set up a time to meet so they could talk about us. Her parents were so relieved to hear about our family. They had put their only child on a plane to the U.S. for nine months with very little information about our family. God totally orchestrated everything. We spent time with our Korean friends every Friday night while stationed in Korea. They had been in our home and we had been in theirs. As a parent, what situation could have possibly been any better? As a mother of eight, I was so thankful our friends could give Hyo-Jin's parents a sense of peace about where she was going to live and a character reference for Rich and me, as parents.

God knew exactly what our family needed to test our hearts in the area of surrendering all. We found it was easy to talk about but much harder to live it out. We learned what it really meant to love someone unconditionally as Hyo-Jin came into our family. We offered our home, our time, and our very lives, to love a perfect stranger. In time Hyo-Jin became our ninth daughter as well as another sister to the rest of our girls. Our family is still involved in her life today.

Our family vision to demonstrate God's love by making the most of every opportunity is what has made us a strong military family. Even after twenty-two years of active-duty service, our family made the decision to endure a one-year, unaccompanied tour. We had prayed many months in advance for the opportunity for my husband to command a brigade. When the list was released, my husband had been chosen to command Joint Task Force Bravo in Honduras. It certainly wasn't what we had hoped for, but we believed God was in control.

We are currently one month into our year apart, and we know God has a purpose for our family this year, in two different locations. We are so grateful for our military lifestyle. We see and embrace it as one big opportunity.

CHAPTER 5
ANOTHER MOVE

Now the Lord said to Abram: Get out of your country, from your family, and from your Father's house, to a land that I will show you.

Genesis 12:1

Look, the Lord your God has set the land before you; go up and posses it, as the Lord God of your fathers has spoken to you; do not fear or be discouraged.

Deuteronomy 1:21

Experience has taught me that each move brings with it a roller coaster full of emotion. The uphill ride is like the feelings of excitement and anticipation of another new adventure. Approaching the top, knowing there is a significant drop, yet unable to turn back, is comparable to the feelings of fear and uncertainty to leave special friends and our current home to begin again when there is nothing we can do about it. Looking forward to the fun of every curve, upside-down loop and the wild corkscrews is the best way to get the most out of the ride or we can choose to hang on tight, keep our eyes closed and hate the whole experience. This is comparable to our attitude to face another move choosing to enjoy the experience or hate every minute of it.

As with most of the difficult aspects of military life, God knew how easy it would be to let the frequent moves rule me and steal my joy. Instead, in one of my quiet times just prior to one of our moves, God's word from Deuteronomy 1:21 gave me a completely new perspective toward the prospect of moving again. It says, "The Lord has given a new land to us and we are to posses it and not to be afraid or discouraged." I now consider each new place to be the new land that God has decided to send our family. It has included our new home, new neighborhood, and new friends. When I finally began to realize that God was in control of each duty assignment it gave me new hope for my future (Jeremiah 31:17), and I was no longer anxious when I heard the words "new duty assignment."

Our family has experienced the many challenges and benefits of moving ten times in twenty-two years of active-duty service! As we have experienced the practical and emotional challenges of moving, I have been encouraged as I remember that "Faith is the substance of things hoped for, the evidence of things not seen" (Hebrews 11:1). Pending a move, I remind myself daily that God has control of our lives, and I can absolutely trust Him with the details of our next move! In May

2003 we divided our home into three separate shipments of accompanied baggage, unaccompanied baggage and household items for storage until we returned to the United States. We were on our way to spend two years in South Korea. Initially the housing director was not going to approve our joint travel orders as the new housing for families at Camp Humphreys, Korea, was not yet complete. We were disappointed but we knew God was in control. We began to pray for an open door. Within a few days we heard from a dear friend already living in Korea and working on Camp Humphreys. He had arranged for our entire family to move into an apartment above a Christian organization called the Hospitality House. It was within walking distance of the front gate. Our part was to agree to help support the ministry with a few other couples until permanent missionaries arrived. We immediately agreed and the housing director gave us the permission needed to travel together as a family. This was our first overseas move, so trusting God for the smallest of details became absolutely essential. Packing only what was necessary became our motto. We traveled from Fort Campbell, Kentucky, cross country in our van to our final departing destination of Seattle, Washington. We were able to spend a wonderful week with dear friends near Seattle before we left the U.S. We chose a plane departing at 1:00 AM flying direct from Seattle to Osan Air Force Base. We thought it was a great plan so the children would be able to sleep much of the way. As we approached the check-in desk we met a line of soldiers and airmen that seemed to be a mile long! I looked at my husband and then turned to our children to encourage them. Our youngest had already found a spot to sleep on top of our eighteen pieces of luggage. My husband soon returned to take everything but our carry-on bags. Eventually he returned with the news that our plane was delayed. I felt like the worst mother in the world as I watched our girls trudge exhausted through the airport. It was then that I realized we were leaving the country for two years! I began to pray, asking God to help me to not worry but rest in His provision for what lay ahead. Korea turned out to be one of our most cherished assignments. God had totally prepared the way. We arrived in Osan, South Korea, to a warm welcome, a beautiful apartment and immediate friendships. I could not have prayed for anything more.

As a military spouse, I recognize that each move will have its ups and downs, but I remind myself I am the example my children will watch as they decide whether or not to embrace each new place as home. Making our new house our home begins by unpacking every box and hanging every picture. Most importantly it includes opening up my heart to new people, experiences, and more everlasting friendships.

We recently completed our tenth move in twenty-two years of active-duty service, I contemplated the important question… "What is home?" The move was a very unusual one for us. It was our first door-to-door move. The packers finished packing the truck on a Thursday in the late afternoon. The next morning, after finishing the final housekeeping chores in our old home, we loaded up our van and truck for the convoy to Norfolk, Virginia. Our household goods were to be delivered the following Monday morning. We thought this was going to be our easiest move. Our plan was to receive our household goods on Monday, unpack as much as we could on Tuesday, and start our drive to visit family and friends in three different states on Wednesday. It sounded like a great plan until we arrived in Norfolk, completely exhausted. I thought, "What were we thinking? How can we leave with the house a wreck, only to return from vacation to finish the work?" Then it hit me. "Would it really feel like home when we returned?" With only a few nights to spend in our new house, I began to meditate once again on the question… "What really makes each new house a home?"

As I considered our moves over the last twenty-two years, I came to a conclusion. Home is where we live together and decide to plant ourselves and invest our lives. Home is where I have purpose in my heart to live as if it were permanent, instead of living as if it were temporary, just waiting for the next move.

Yet living in the past can be just as counterproductive. I realized that I have a choice to make each time we move. Am I willing to put my whole heart into our new home, knowing God has chosen it for our family, or will I continue to live in the past? Will I long for the life we had at our previous duty assignment or will I allow God to fill me with excitement for what He has for us as we move and put down roots again? When God wants to bless me I have found that it is often my own attitude that keeps me from experiencing the full measure of what the Lord has for me. I have two examples from my own journey that taught me that making somewhere home is truly tied to the focus of my heart.

In June 1998, we left Fort Campbell, Kentucky, to spend a year at Fort Leavenworth, Kansas, as my husband attended the Command and General Staff College Course. Our departure was a painful goodbye, leaving our home and the friendships we had shared for over five years. The children and I cried as we drove away. My husband asked me why I was crying. He reminded me he was actually going to be home for a whole year while he was in school. I knew in my heart this was a great reason to rejoice, yet my heart was breaking as we backed out of our driveway, away from our dear friends, and our life at Fort Campbell. I realized that Fort Campbell, our fourth duty station, really had become home. Even though this was one of the most challenging duty assignments for us as a family, due to many separations, it really was home. As a family we did not just endure it or just survive until we could get out of there. We had planted ourselves in our neighborhood, our church, in the community, and in the soldiers and families who were part of the 160th Special Operations Aviation Regiment. It was home!

In the thirty-first chapter of Jeremiah, God gives me several powerful promises. He tells me that He has replenished every sorrowful soul. He speaks of His everlasting love for me. He says, "I have drawn you and again I will build you and you shall be rebuilt." As we drove to Fort Leavenworth, God kept reminding me of the power of the promise… "Again I will rebuild you, and you shall be rebuilt." As those thoughts sunk in and as I prayed, my heavy heart changed to one of anticipation for the year ahead.

I had a choice. Was I going to let go and rest, trusting God with our new assignment to Fort Leavenworth, Kansas, and all He had for us there? Or was I going to long for the life we were leaving?

We arrived at Fort Leavenworth and God again demonstrated His faithfulness. We were assigned housing in one of the nicest neighborhoods. Our home was a new home, with a huge fenced-in back yard, on a cul-de-sac. God reminded us of His love for us by assigning housing to one of our dearest friends, right behind us. He even answered the simplest prayer request I made for a clothes line in the back yard.

These things were just the beginning of the wonderful year God had planned for us. My husband's schedule allowed him to be home every day for breakfast and arrive home early enough to play outside with our girls before dinner. He had time to coach two of our daughters' soccer teams, and he never missed our eldest daughter's games. Some of our closest friendships were made as we opened our home and made a commitment to love and serve our neighbors. We attended a church in Kansas

City and we were blessed with lifelong friendships. The Lord also allowed us to get to know a few older couples who were a tremendous encouragement to us. As our year at Leavenworth was coming to a close, I was reminded of what I may have missed if I had chosen to live in the past at Fort Campbell, instead of trusting God for what He had for us at Fort Leavenworth.

I am sure you have similar stories to tell. A precious friend of mine, shares her story so beautifully.

Being flexible has never been something that has come easily for me. God, being the wonderful, all-knowing Father that He is, designed a way for me to be more flexible, able to trust amidst change, new beginnings and unknowns. Marrying Brian, then a captain in the U.S. Army, was the beginning of a journey that would grow me in my walk with Christ in a way that a life outside of the Army may not have so effectively accomplished. From the time I married and moved from Pennsylvania, leaving a job I had for six years, leaving all family and friends and ministry to begin a new life with a start point in Fort Rucker, Alabama, the Lord began to stretch me and I had to trust Him. Just as I began to feel established in one place, we'd move. The two years it took me to make our house a home took only hours to tear down and pack in boxes. The first couple of moves I had asked the questions "How will I ever make friends like I had here?" or "How will we ever find a church like this one or neighbors or a house?" With each move the Lord has provided exactly what we have needed. When we moved to Texas, we rented a house that was over our housing allowance trusting that it was "the house" that the Lord had for us. Within a week of moving in Brian received an unexpected raise that covered the difference of our rent. Then there was the time we moved to Germany with Brian leaving for a one-year deployment within eighteen days of arrival. God provided a street full of Christian sisters that were in the same circumstances to help share the burden of being without our husbands, to say nothing of how I learned to lean on the Lord to be my provider, my sufficiency. When we moved to Colorado our bid on a house was rejected only to find a home that was a much more suitable place for our family. I could tell story after story of God's faithfulness after our nine moves, seven babies, two foreign countries and two lengthy deployments. He is sufficient. He is trustworthy. He cares for His sheep and He is enough. He is mindful of our weaknesses, loves us enough to stretch us by getting us out of our comfort zone and patient with us as we journey.

This life as an army wife has new change around every corner. God has a way of preparing our hearts, if we are willing, for what He has in store. I am learning that around each corner, the Lord is there waiting with His hand outstretched ready to be my All in All. Psalm 16 has become a life verse. Psalm 16:8 & 9 says, "I have set the Lord always before me; because He is at my right hand I shall not be moved.

Therefore my heart is glad, and my glory rejoices; my flesh also will rest in hope." Most likely the twists and turns of life will continue with unexpected moves and assignments. Psalm 16:11 says "You will show me the path of life; In Your presence is fullness of joy; At Your right hand are pleasures forevermore." That is enough to help me rest the next time Brian asks, "How would you like to move to…"

As my friend Deborah's testimony states, the emotional challenges of moving become easier as we learn that God has planned what is best for us and He is with us each step of the way.

God has always used our moves to teach me new things. Our move to Tampa, Florida, following our time at Fort Leavenworth was no exception.

We learned early in the fall of our year at Fort Leavenworth that our follow on assignment was to Mac Dill Air Force Base in Tampa, Florida. It sounded exciting to all of us. It was a place we had never been. Beautiful weather year round and we would be surrounded by choice beaches. After the initial news, I never really thought much more about it. We were having such a wonderful tour at Fort Leavenworth, that I had forgotten the key ingredient to every move, which is prayer. Even though it would be some months before the actual move, I should have been praying. Our sixth daughter was just a month old when our movers started packing our household goods. We were preparing to pack out, drive from Kansas to Maryland to visit family and then to Tampa, Florida, with a newborn, a two-year-old, a four-year-old, a six-year-old, an eight-year-old, and an eleven-year-old. This trip alone should have motivated me to pray. We had decided to rent a home from another military family that my husband already knew. It seemed so simple. We drove up to our new home, in Brandon, Florida, on July 8, 1999. The temperature was 99 degrees Fahrenheit with 100% humidity. As we walked up the sidewalk we were greeted by several lizards. I felt like I was part of the movie *Jurassic Park*! I had never seen such creatures. Of course, my children were trying to catch them. When I reached to unlock the door, I burned my hand on the doorknob. Being tired and hot, my initial thoughts were not good ones! We had just arrived at our new home and I was already longing for Kansas.

We knew in advance that my husband's new job would require him to travel and deploy to the Middle East. What I didn't know was that he would be required to travel within two weeks of our arrival. I remember very vividly the morning I sat at our kitchen table, trying not to cry and wishing we were back at Fort Leavenworth. It was at this point, I realized my huge mistake. I had neglected to pray before our move and now I was struggling to be content in our new home. I learned the hard way that prayer is the key that prepares my heart to say goodbye and to start over again.

As I reflected on what had become a very difficult move for me, I realized a new truth that applies to our lives as military spouses. As always, it involves a choice we have to make. Are we going to keep to ourselves at each new assignment so it does not hurt as much when we PCS again? Or are we going to allow God to use us and teach us, at each new duty assignment. Are we willing to move with our husbands even if it is only for a year? Are we willing to move to the next assignment knowing a deployment is already planned and required? When our heart is to trust God and believe that He has decided the location, duration, and the circumstance of each assignment, it is impossible to move with a bad attitude and to be unthankful when we finally get there.

Before moving to Norfolk, Virginia, my husband and I didn't agree on where to live. The beach home my husband picked was brand new and gorgeous, but I didn't know how I could possibly make our family and our things fit into its design. God quickly reminded me I needed to let go and rest in my husband's decision. The day we moved in, the promised appliances were not in place and the hot water did not work. It would have been so easy to complain and tell my husband "I told you so," but I remembered that God had answered our prayers for my husband to be assigned to one of the two slots available at the Staff College in Norfolk. The enemy wanted to cause me to be unthankful and fight with my husband, causing division and stress in our new home. The enemy hoped I would forget the scripture that encourages me to rejoice always, pray without ceasing, and in everything give thanks for this is the will of God for me (1 Thessalonians 5:16-18). It is a verse I had hidden in my heart years ago to help prepare me for each move. It quickly came to mind as we were trying to decide the best course of action to feed our large family for a few days until our refrigerator was delivered.

As I look back at each duty station, I remembered the tremendous blessing each one has been. Our assignments have blessed us because of our willingness to be planted and to reach out and meet our neighbors, and the soldiers and family members in each new unit. As military families we must accept the challenge that comes with each move and make the effort to get to know our neighbors, plant ourselves and make it home.

How do we prepare for the emotional difficulty of moving? Mary Dailey, wife of Lieutenant General (retired) Dell Dailey, shared with me some thoughts that helped her through many moves and years of service.

"We believe that in our wedding vows when we swore before God that we would support each other for better and for worse...that really meant when the packers come to the house. Those vows should have read something more like... 'In sickness and in health, for richer and for poorer, and when the packers come to your house to move all of your worldly goods to a place you've never heard of before!'"

Her words reminded me that moving is not easy, but it is part of the commitment I made when I married my soldier. I quickly learned that saying goodbye to dear friends brings feelings of sadness and pain, but God quickly replaces it with an excitement that looks forward to the new adventure ahead. We know it will be filled with new friends, experiences, and places to explore.

As I have wrestled with the emotional roller coaster of moving, it helps me to remember that I cannot doubt God's plan for our lives. "For I know the plans I have for you," declares the Lord, "plans to prosper you and not to harm you, plans to give you hope and a future" (Jeremiah 29:11). As I shared in my story of our move from Fort Leavenworth to Tampa, I quickly forgot the truth that God had a plan for us. My first day in Tampa felt like the desert of Egypt to me. My attitude became one of whining and complaining. This was not helping my family adjust to our new home. The Lord taught me through the following scriptures. Hebrews 12:2 speaks of the time when Israel was delivered out of Egypt and then led into the Sinai Desert, where they forgot the miracles of God. They began to whine and complain. They actually wanted to go back to Egypt, just like I wanted to go back to Fort Leavenworth. Can you imagine that? I knew the Biblical example and had many examples from my own life that God is faithful, yet I longed to go back to what was comfortable and safe. It seemed easier than trusting God for something even better in our new location. The lesson I learned is that I cannot look back from where we have come! This is not to say that we are to forget the past…in fact God wants us to remember what he has done in us and through us. But to look back with a yearning when God is calling us to a new land is dangerous, as Lot's wife found out as she looked back in Sodom and was transformed into a pillar of salt (Genesis 19:26).

Psalm 106 tells of a time when the Israelites doubted God, by taking the things He had already done for them for granted. I wondered how many times I had forgotten the wonderful things God had done for us at each previous assignment. It says, The Israelites soon forgot all God had done and they did not wait for His counsel....

With every move, there is a time of transition and waiting. It requires patience. It takes time to settle in, find your way around, and begin to get involved. Knowing this helps us to look forward to our new home, trusting God, knowing He has the absolute BEST for us! His best includes the precious relationships He has in store for us at each new place. For us many of these relationships have become lifelong friendships. In fact, as we traveled cross country prior to flying to Korea in 2003, we had the pleasure of staying with three different families before leaving the United States. Our girls were excited to rekindle old friendships but the experience motivated them to seek new ones when we arrived in Korea. As a military family we love the opportunity to have friends all over the world. This is another blessing we remember as we prepare to move again.

I often remind my children that God is preparing them for

something exciting. Not every child or young adult has the opportunity to experience life as our children have. They have traveled the U.S. and the world, learned to quickly make new friends, and they know and appreciate the cost of freedom. The following are two testimonies from our seventeen- and fifteen-year-old daughters.

Hannah, seventeen, writes, *"The love I have for the military and my country is found in the depths of my heart. I didn't choose to be born into a military family and to take on the weight and uncertainty that it can sometimes entail. But I can say one thing for sure; I did make the choice to commit my heart to supporting my dad and my country. I have chosen to accept the military lifestyle.*

"One of the hardest things about being a military family is the constant picking up and moving. I can remember that when I was little I couldn't wait to hear where we were moving next. What new place was I going to see? What new people would I meet? It was the anticipation of a little girl, who didn't know any other kind of life. But as I got older, moving became very difficult. I found myself dreading our next move even before we had gotten settled at our new duty station. It was so easy to simply close my heart to the thought of getting 'planted.' What was the point? Why should I get attached, only to be torn from it a year or two down the road. I found it easier to close myself off and become hardhearted, rather than to try to make it 'home.'

"It was then that I realized the tremendous mistake I was making. It's true I had been given no choice as to whether or not I wanted to live the military lifestyle. The fact is that I was chosen by God to live the military lifestyle. The only person who could see where this path was taking me had my best interest at heart. My Creator had decided. Jesus Christ, the one person who loved me more than anything else, had chosen. He had created me to walk this path. So, I had a choice to make. Would I continue to walk in self-pity and become hard hearted? Or would I choose to live each day, looking for the joy, opportunity, and blessings that were mine for the taking? Would I choose to walk down the path that was laid for me, with a surrendered and joyful heart?

"It was at this point in my life that I made the choice to make the most of my life as a soldier's daughter. I began to see things in a very different light. I was amazed at how much the Lord was teaching me through my trials. The best part was that once I surrendered my heart to His calling, He began to bless me in unimaginable ways. My life became a true joy. I made many dear friends and the Lord settled my heart at my new home.

"The true test came when once again it was time to pick up and move. I won't tell you that I was overjoyed and that I wasn't sad. I would have to say that the most recent move we made was the hardest for me. However, the amazing thing was that through my sadness I felt a peace that I had never experienced before. Somehow I just knew that I was going to be ok. I placed

my full trust in the Lord and once more said goodbye to all I had come to hold dear. We packed up and headed out into the unknown. But this time I held the promise that even though I didn't know what that future held, my Lord did, and that was all that mattered."

Mary, fifteen, shares one of the things God taught her through moving: *"As a military daughter, moving has always been a part of my life. I don't know what it is like to have a hometown or to have the same friends for more than three years. My whole life has been about change; changing homes, changing friends, changing places. As a little girl, moving was an adventure. It was always something to look forward to, and from the eyes of a six-year-old, it was the highlight of my summers. It was fun to pack up and move into another home, but as I got older moving became much harder. With each move, there was still the same sense of a new adventure ahead but it was accompanied by a sadness of leaving my old life behind. I began to plant myself at each new duty station and every time we had to move, I felt like I was being uprooted, yet again, leaving a piece of my heart behind. I know what it is like to drive away from the place that used to be my home with tears in my eyes, wondering why I once more had to be taken away from the life I had come to love.*

"Our most recent move, from Fayetteville, North Carolina, to Norfolk, Virginia, was the most difficult for me personally. In Fayetteville, we attended a great church, and had incredible

friends. It was definitely not a place I wanted to leave, but once again I picked up my life and moved away. I moved up to Virginia about a month after my family, due to my participation in a short-term mission trip. By the time I got to Norfolk, my family had already become accustomed to their new lives, but I was still missing the life I had left behind. I felt like no one could relate to what I was feeling, not even my family, because they had already made Virginia their home. They all seemed content, yet I was still struggling with all that I had left behind and there was still pain from uprooting and leaving the relationships that I had come to hold very dear. There were many tear-filled mornings of crying out to the Lord for strength and a joy to make it through the day.

"One morning, I came across Proverbs 10:30, which says, 'The righteous will never be uprooted.' I couldn't help but think how amazing it would be to never have to be uprooted, how great it would be to live in one house, and have all my friends right there with me. It was then that I heard the Lord quietly say that He couldn't promise me that I wouldn't have to be uprooted and move again. Life as a soldier's daughter is what He has called me to, it is who I am. I can't simply walk away from my Creator's plan for my life. Again, I heard the Lord quietly speak to my heart, saying that even though He couldn't promise that I wouldn't have to move again, He could promise that no matter where I go, or what I have to leave behind, I will never have to be uprooted from my Creator. I

realized in that moment the promise of Proverbs 10:30, that no matter where I am uprooted from, I will never be uprooted from my Lord. I will NEVER be taken away from my heart's greatest desire. Wherever I am, I will always be rooted into the true source of life that brings me joy and contentment in the place that I have been planted!"

The words of my daughters make me so thankful for this lifestyle. Although each move has its challenges and painful goodbyes, it has been through these experiences that our family has grown the most.

We moved to Fort Eustis, Virginia, in May 2008. It wasn't without glitches, but once again, God was faithful to help us stay calm and focused. We are waiting expectantly to see what God is going to teach us and the opportunities that will come from living in our new home. It is hard to imagine any other journey then the one we are on as a military family.

CHAPTER 6
THE WAITING

Let us hold fast the confession of our hope without wavering, for He who promised is faithful.
Hebrews 10:23

On September 11, 2001, our country was struck by a terrorist attack. Within a span of forty-five minutes, the World Trade Center buildings and the Pentagon were struck by large commercial aircraft, which exploded on impact. We watched in total shock, as the events unfolded on television. How could this be happening in America? The immensity of the tragedy began to sink in as we realized that thousands of innocent lives were lost in the attacks on the World Trade Centers and the Pentagon.

Our reaction to the horrific attacks progressed from complete disbelief to sadness, then fear, and finally anger. Slowly, on U.S. military installations all over the world, a second realization began to enter the hearts and mind of military spouses. We knew it would be our warriors who would be called upon to ensure that this act of terror did not go unpunished.

We probably all remember what we were doing that morning of September 11, 2001. We are a home-schooling family and so on that morning we were just finishing our breakfast and devotion time when my neighbor called and said, "Turn on the television, quick!" The girls and I ran to turn it on and sat in disbelief as we watched the Twin Towers burning. Then within minutes, the news of the attack on the Pentagon was announced! I said, "Girls, we have to pray." We were afraid and very sad. At the time our girls were thirteen, ten, eight, six, five, and two. We sat on the floor and began to ask God for His help. I knew it was the only thing we could do. We continued to pray throughout the morning, hoping for any word from my husband. Eventually, he called and said, "I don't know when I will be home, but I love you and the girls very much."

Our time of waiting began. We didn't know what was going to happen next. In a few short hours, people's lives changed forever. One day rolled into the next due to the hours of work required of my husband and all those in uniform. At the time we were stationed in Tampa, Florida, assigned to United States Central Command. Central Command, responsible for planning and conducting military operations in South West Asia, including Afghanistan, became a very busy place. I knew that it was just a matter of time before my husband would deploy.

Key scriptures came to mind that encouraged our family to pray for those in authority. We decided now was the time to pray fervently for our president and for the men and women fulfilling roles of leadership for our country. We knew the decisions they would make that day and in the weeks and months to follow would impact our lives as a military family and our nation. James 5:16 says, "The fervent prayer of a righteous man avails much." Oh how our family prayed, that day and in the many weeks that followed. It was during this time that we learned what the word "wait" really meant. The little time we had together was difficult, as the uncertainty of war loomed over us. We waited each day for deployment orders. The girls and I began to pray for all the men and women who would be called upon to defend our nation. We also prayed for the families who like us would support and wait for their soldier, sailor, airman, or marine from the other front…the home front. We continued running daily to God to ask for His mercy and to find grace to help in our time of need (Heb 4:16). We were certainly needy. At times, I felt helpless. I often thought of Jonah and how he must have felt immediately after being swallowed by a whale. His reaction to his circumstance was to pray. It was a wonderful example to me. It quickly reminded me of Psalm 73:25-26, that says, "Whom have I in heaven but You? And there is none upon earth that I desire besides you. My flesh and my heart fail; But God is my strength and my portion forever." I clung to these verses, as I had no idea what the future would hold.

The weeks following the horrible attacks were very difficult. Our family experienced a painful time of waiting. Headlines like "The U.S. Military Heads to South West Asia" served as a reminder of pending deployment. It was not too long before our deepest concern became reality. The two questions that were heavily on my heart were when would my husband deploy and how long would he be gone? As a military family it has always been very difficult to not know the exact time or day when we will have to kiss the one we hold most precious, and tell him "goodbye." It is then that our family must once again live life, waiting for his safe return. As a military spouse, it was sometimes very hard to think or pray past our own needs and situation. But I began to learn that God wanted our family to pray for the bigger picture of what He would do. The Scripture tells us in Romans 8:28, "And we know that in all things God works for the good of those who love him; who have been called according to his purpose." From Jonah's example and other times in our lives, we knew God could take any situation and help us to grow through it as we kept our eyes on Him. We also believed God could take the worst situation and use it for good. The girls and I spoke of the many examples that were evident within days following the 9/11 attacks. As we lived through the events of 9/11, we thanked God daily for the amazing change in the hearts of those in our nation. The horrific situation had brought our nation together. We discussed the events taking place as people were demonstrating their compassion and concern for one another. Each Friday as we made our commissary run to MacDill AFB, we passed dozens of patriotic Americans standing on a corner, waving flags and holding signs with words of encouragement and thanks to our men and women in uniform. Even though our lives were in turmoil, our girls expressed pride in their daddy every time we passed by that crowd of faithful Americans.

As a family, we were touched by these demonstrations of love and support for our nation and for those in uniform. We discussed how we would expect this kind of support in a "military town" like Clarksville, Tennessee; Tampa, Florida; or Fayetteville, North Carolina, but what about the small town or city in America that is not close to a military installation? Since that time, I have been encouraged as a military spouse as we have visited such places, including my hometown of Stoughton, Wisconsin. The girls and I were downtown shopping and experienced words of thanks for our military and to us a military family, as we also have sacrificed so much in the fight for freedom.

These words of thanks helped us as we were waiting. It was like a nugget of encouragement from the Lord. He did not want our family to walk in the fear of the unknown but to trust Him and His promises for our situation. Our hope was built on the fact that God was continually with us (Psalm 73:23). It was because of this promise that we gained a sense of peace and strength! As a military spouse I have learned to be honest with God. Whether I express my feelings aloud or not, God already knows my heart. Over the years I have used a daily journal to help me convey thanks to God as well as my burdens. I have taught our older daughters to do the same. We have memorized the scripture that tells us to be anxious for nothing, but in everything by prayer and supplication, with thanksgiving, to let our requests be made known to God, and His peace will guard our heart and mind, in Christ Jesus (Philippians 4:6-7). Many times after my husband deployed to Afghanistan, I would find one of our daughters crying. Their concern for their dad was overwhelming them. I would encourage them to take their emotion and use it for good. We would immediately begin to pray for their daddy and the men and women serving with him. It was amazing to watch God take their hurting heart and restore a sense of peace as they gave their burdens to Him.

My husband deployed on November 11, 2001, Veterans Day, two months after the September 11th attacks. He was off to fight the war on terrorism. What a painful, heavy- hearted, long day for all of us. At the time, we had six daughters who loved their father very dearly. We were all dreading the goodbye. As the hours drew near for him to depart, we knew there was nothing we could do to stop him from leaving! I asked God to help me be strong for my husband and for my children, yet on the inside my heart was breaking. As my husband gave his last hug to one of our daughters, I knew I was next. I quickly prayed asking God to help me be courageous.

Ecclesiastes 11:5 says, "As you do not know what the way of the wind is, or how the bones grow in the womb of her who is with child, so you do not know the works of God who makes everything. As my husband waved his last goodbye and began walking away from us I told God I didn't know what He was doing but I would trust Him with the outcome and be faithful with whatever work He had for me during our time apart. I continue to ask God for a passion and willingness to be in the middle of His plan for our lives, even if His plan is difficult or emotionally painful. Such a time happened in my own life while my husband deployed. I was newly pregnant with our seventh daughter. In the weeks that followed, my bout with extreme morning sickness, or in my case, all-day sickness, set in. It was so intense my girlfriends began cooking small meals for the girls and me. I was so sick that my husband asked his father to come and take us all back to Maryland after he left. The time with Rich's parents was just what I needed, and after staying with them for over a month, I finally began to feel better. My morning sickness had faded and I had a new burst of energy. Each day was much brighter as I could function normally. I actually looked forward to cooking and eating again. It was almost Christmas. We had the option of staying with my in-laws throughout the holidays but for some reason I felt led to be in our own home for Christmas. During one of our infrequent and short phone calls, I told my husband my heart. He had his reservations but he finally gave his blessing to let us travel home alone. It was a very tough decision to make because we enjoyed being with Rich's parents very much. I was also worried about how the girls would react to my decision. Our girls were between the ages of two and thirteen, and thankfully they handled the news very well. They did not beg me to stay with their grandparents, even though they would have loved to, but instead they supported my decision. I was so proud of them.

We arrived home with just a few weeks before Christmas. With my new energy and appetite, it was so much fun to begin our traditional baking and decorating the house. I felt it was important for our traditions to go on even if my husband was away. Due to our circumstance we decided to keep Christmas simple. We began a new family tradition of exchanging names and giving small gifts to one another. There was a five-dollar spending limit and the gift also had to include something handmade. This part of the gift could be a simple hand written letter to something handcrafted. It was also during this time that the Lord impressed upon me that while my husband was gone, the girls and I had extra time to bless others. We baked extra goodies and went door to door early on Christmas Eve to hand out what we had made and sing a rendition of "We Wish You a Merry Christmas." Our time ended with the girls reciting Luke 2:1-14 which they had diligently memorized. The girls and I also decided our weekly visit to the assisted living home would be done on Christmas Day. On Christmas morning we opened our homemade gifts. Each thoughtful gift touched our hearts in a new way. I saw the excitement in our daughters as they could not wait to give their gift away. We left for the assisted living home and spent the morning going room to room, singing Christmas carols as the girls gave away their prized Beanie Babies. The morning was spent loving people we didn't even know, yet we left as the ones who had been blessed. We certainly were missing having our soldier at home, but we recognized that God was doing a new work in all of us. Ever since then we have tried to spend part of Christmas Day doing the same thing. God used our time apart to reveal His plan for the Juergens family each Christmas. We are so grateful for every Christmas together, but now we are not devastated if God decides we should be apart.

I want to share one last example of how God used that very difficult time for good. He allowed my husband to find time every few days to send a family devotion home, via e-mail. My husband sent so many, I had to number each one to keep them in order. I saw God doing a work in our daughters' hearts, as well as my own. We experienced the power of a father's teaching, even as we were half a world apart. God again used our situation for good. It is now seven years later, and my husband has been deployed three more times in support of the War on Terrorism. Again, as a military spouse I don't know what will be requested of me in the future, but I trust that God

DIANA JUERGENS

does! My burden to write a book to encourage military spouses began a few weeks before 9/11. I did not know how I could accomplish such a task, but I quickly realized God's timing was perfect. God had me ready to journal as September 11th unfolded. I was able to capture my thoughts and feelings to represent all military spouses, during a very tragic time in our history.

As the wife of a soldier I have learned to support my husband in his military profession. I have found the best way to do this is by asking God for His help to respond properly to whatever circumstances are placed upon me and our family. Just recently my husband called to tell me his departure date for his unaccompanied tour may be moved up by one week. A week does not sound like a big deal until you throw in a PCS move for our family of ten, a high school graduation as well as my husband's graduation from the Joint Forces Staff College. God gave me the ability to respond with few words and wait on Him for the outcome. Whether in times of peace or times of war, my husband leaves us for extended amounts of time, either to train or fight for freedom. As a mother of eight military children I have the tough and painful job of helping them cope with constant separations. In times like today, I not only help them through the normal challenges of being a military child, but must also help them deal with fears that come with deployments to dangerous war zones. I quickly learned God was truly the only source for their fears. Fifteen years ago as we began homeschooling, my husband put one requirement on my life as the teacher. He told me that I must spend time in God's word and pray with the children every day. I believe this has been our children's strong tower as they have had to wait so many times for the safe return of their daddy and for what the future may hold. We have seen the fruit of this as each of our girls has a spirit of prayer. Even our youngest at two and a half will not get down from the table without having her turn to pray. As we wait on the next deployment I must prepare my heart and our children's hearts to say goodbye. Our younger girls have asked me, "How can we possibly prepare to say goodbye to Dad?" I explained in our own strength we organize and plan. We are currently preparing to move as my husband leaves the country for one year without us. I have told them our friends and at times the unit Family Readiness Group can help with the practical needs we will face, but God is the only answer to help us with our emotional and spiritual needs. Running to Him for comfort and courage was the only support we would need as we prepared our hearts to say goodbye again.

I often communicate to our daughters that it is through God's word that He gives us promises directly from His own heart. It has brought us comfort believing what the scripture says in Deuteronomy 31:6 and Hebrews 13:5, "I will never leave you nor forsake you." Knowing God is always with us has helped us to walk through the toughest situations. For our family, the requirement on our lives to wait for the time of that next deployment or waiting until our soldier comes home again, have been two of the toughest challenges we have faced.

My husband is leaving in June 2008 for a one-year unaccompanied tour to Honduras. Once again as he leaves we know we must endure the same waiting and unknown. We do not know what the future holds, but as the famous old hymn "Because He Lives" says, we do know the one who holds the future. We know God is always there for us. We have committed to trust and rely on Him, (Psalms 31) as we wait for and experience the next events He has chosen for our lives.

CHAPTER 7
THE PAINFUL GOODBYES

When my soul fainted within me, I remembered
the Lord.
Jonah 2:7

As I write, the men and women in uniform are deployed
more than ever before. The War on Terror has been going on for
seven years. What does this mean to the military spouse and
family? It means many painful goodbyes.

One such goodbye happened in our own family as we
returned from two years of command in Korea. This was to be
my husband's first deployment in almost two years. We knew
the day he was leaving; in fact, we knew months in advance that
he would be leaving. Yet it didn't make the goodbye any easier.

It felt like such a sacrifice to walk through another painful
goodbye. This was to be our fourth separation due to a real-
world deployment. How was God going to use this in our lives?
I knew it was His plan but I continued to ask myself, "How

many more times can I do this? How many more times can the children bear the pain?"

I began praying about the painful goodbye and our time apart, months in advance. Where was my peace? My husband's heart was broken as he prepared to say goodbye to me and our eight daughters. Our youngest daughter was just three weeks old. I remember very clearly the thoughts that ran through my mind that morning. I knew I had a choice to make. Was I going to be sad, angry and embittered by another deployment or was I going to choose to run to God and believe His promises? My heart was overwhelmed, but I chose to give my burdens to God knowing He is my rock, shelter and strong tower (Psalm 61:1-3). Encouraging my girls to do the same was critical. We had to purpose in our hearts to keep the enemy from robbing us of our joy! The Bible story of Daniel allowed me to remember that if I chose God's way it would lead to what is the absolutely best for us, even when our hearts didn't like our situation, as we were facing another deployment.

The dreaded day came and all that was left to do was to take my soldier to the airport. We decided it would be best if he said goodbye to our children at home and only I would drop him off, since our older girls were able to stay and watch their younger sisters. After a painful time of kissing and holding each daughter, we got in the car. I will never forget the pain I felt as our daughters stood in the driveway, trying to be brave, holding onto one another and waving to their daddy with tears streaming down their faces. I was angry. I was thinking, "Where is family when you need them? Where is our support to help us through this very painful time?" As we started to drive, I began to pray, asking God for His help. I was angry about not having any support, but as I confessed this to my husband, the Lord reminded me of a tremendous scripture verse that applied to our situation. In Ecclesiastes 7:3, it says, "Sorrow is better than laughter for by a sad countenance, the heart is made better." When I returned home an hour later, I heard my girls' testimonies of how their hearts were breaking as we drove away. After our car was out of sight, they had gone into the house and had gathered together, cried and prayed. They said they knew the Lord was the only one who could help them. As a parent, I realized that morning's painful goodbye had taught our daughters a priceless lesson. At their young and tender ages, they had learned to run to the Lord for help. If family had been there, they may not have turned to the Lord for their comfort, strength, peace and joy. It took their words to help me realize my anger was useless, for God had His plan. He was the support we needed. He used that painful morning to draw our children closer to Him. As a mother, could I possibly have chosen for it not to happen, to protect them from the pain, and have them miss that tremendous lesson of faith?

Without the physical support of friends or family we had to choose to run to God with our hurting hearts. This was the absolute best lesson we could ever have learned. During the first phone call from my husband, with tears running down my face, I shared the story of how the girls had prayed. We thanked the Lord together for our situation and for what He had already taught us. We decided that if this was the only lesson we would learn from this deployment, it was worth it.

Weeks before my husband left, I began reading scriptures that encouraged me as our family approached another difficult goodbye and time of separation. I knew it would only make a difference if I chose to believe it. As I read Ephesians 6:10, which says, "Be strong in the Lord and in the power of his might," and Nehemiah 8:10 that says, "The joy of the Lord is my strength," I had to decide to ask God to help me apply these verses now in my own life and teach them to our children. As my heart was hurting, I had to continue to cry out to God. "Help me, show me your purpose for our time apart, and give me your peace and strength."

The day before my husband left, in my quiet time with the Lord, I read Ephesians 4:1, which encouraged me to walk worthy of the life to which I had been called. My life was encircled around the life of my soldier. I also read Corinthians 5:15, which reminded me that Jesus died for me so that I should no longer live for myself, but for Him. These verses challenged me to remember, my life and our children's lives were not our own, but God's. Even in the midst of another painful goodbye I had to acknowledge that God had proven to me many times

His plan and purpose for each difficult situation. This was another opportunity to trust and wait on Him.

I kept telling myself it was a privilege to be chosen as part of the plan! I could not see the big picture, but God could. In the weeks prior to my husband's deployment, I had begun to pray for opportunities that would result from our obedience to bear another painful goodbye.

A few weeks after my husband left, I received a phone call from a young military spouse. She had actually worked with my husband in a previous assignment. While together at Fort Campbell, we had spent time with her and her husband, encouraging them as a newly married couple. It was now two years later and we were both now stationed at Fort Bragg, North Carolina. She asked if she could come for a visit and I immediately said yes. I was so excited at the thought to reconnect with her and get to know her children. We quickly set a time and date to meet in our home. Marie called a few days later to ask if she could bring a few friends. They were also young military spouses, seeking encouragement as young wives and mothers. Our initial meeting turned into a weekly Bible study and time of encouragement. My older daughters got involved by helping to care for the children and preparing delicious treats. It became a family event of giving and growing. I was able to dedicate the time needed because my husband was deployed. I quickly realized it was all a part of God's bigger plan for our time a part. Although it was difficult, our separation allowed my daughters and me to invest in these young women and their children. A large part of this was encouraging them in their role as military spouses.

Currently our family is preparing to face another painful goodbye, as my husband leaves for a one-year unaccompanied tour to Honduras. My heart is already experiencing feelings of grief as I know how much we will all miss my husband. The children and I have already begun asking God to help us through our time apart. I have told them waiting until the day he leaves will be too late to prepare their hearts. A few verses that are helping us are found in the first chapter of James. God is reminding us to count it all joy, as we walk through this trial of separation because He will use it to do His "perfect work" in us. As we know God has decided this time for our family to be apart, we must trust Him for the outcome (Proverbs 3:5-6). My heart is to be the example as I teach these truths to our children. We know we cannot avoid the painful day of saying goodbye, but we can prepare for it by continuing to acknowledge that God is faithful and trustworthy. The day my husband leaves we will begin journaling what God is doing in us and through us. We know it will not be easy to be apart, but we know it will be a life-changing experience for all of us. All we have to do is be committed and faithful to do the work God has for us and rejoice in Him (Habakkuk3:18), even when our hearts are heavy and hurting.

CHAPTER 8
RESTING IN GOD'S PEACE

And He said, "My Presence will go with you,
and I will give you rest."

Exodus 33:4

Lord, you will establish peace for us, for you
have also done all our work in us.

Isaiah 26:12

It was a long restless night. Sleeping was difficult. I couldn't
stop thinking about my husband. Was he okay? Were his men
okay? It's been months since I've held him in my arms. When
will I see him again? Will I see him again? And if that wasn't
enough to worry about…what will today bring? Are the kids
going to be okay? What's going to break that I can't fix? Please
don't let it be the computer or the car. Help me, Lord!!

I suspect that my anxious thoughts are not unique. I know
that the Lord wants me to rest in His peace but it is often easier
said than done. Yet somehow I think it is one of the key
principles the Lord is trying to teach me. I have experienced

two great challenges to resting in God's peace since my husband became a special operations soldier. The first is the fear of the unknown that is a part of each deployment. The second is unexpected crises that seem to arise only while my husband is away.

I first experienced the fear of the unknown in 1993, as my husband became a Nightstalker, in the 160th Special Aviation Operations Regiment. The mission of the unit often required unexpected deployments, and the family members were given very little knowledge about what was going on. We could watch the news and speculate, but we rarely knew for sure where the unit was located. Within a few days of a deployment, the rear detachment would hold a briefing to tell us as much as they could, but because of operational security this was often not very much. They would also give us a point of contact for any emergencies that might arise. Communication was infrequent, if at all. In 1993 e-mail was just starting to be used as an effective means of communication. I would check the computer many times a day hoping to find at least a few words from my husband. My heart would sink when there was nothing there. It was so hard to not know when I might hear from him. This was also before cell phones were widely available so moving beyond hearing distance of our home phone was something I never did lightly. I never wanted to miss one of his calls. As a spouse in the 160th we knew that secrecy was an absolute must, due to security reasons, but the reality of why it was necessary didn't make it any easier to live in the "fear of the unknown."

It was during this time that I had to learn to rest in God's peace. I don't think I would have survived in the 160th in support of my soldier without the peace of the Lord. I had to remind myself that God was my refuge and strength. I had to trust God for my husband's safety and peace as well as my own. One of things that really helped was when I asked my husband to journal whenever he was away from us. Having a written record of all that the Lord did was proof for our girls that God works all things for good (Romans 8:28). As they battled their own feelings of loneliness and the sadness of not having Dad around, I wanted them to see God's purpose in every separation. My husband would come home and share his journal entries with me and our girls. They became foundations of faith for us as we learned that the Lord was with each of us even though we were half a world apart.

Due to the nature of the profession my husband has chosen, I have experienced many unexpected, sometimes tragic situations. While in company command, in the 160th, we experienced such an event. Most of the men were away on a training mission. It was the middle of the night when the phone rang. I was afraid to answer it, but I knew I had to. Something had happened and I needed to be at a briefing at 3:00 AM at the battalion headquarters. Unfortunately, I had not planned for such an event. I had no one to call at that time of night to come and stay with our four young daughters and so I had to wait until morning to find out anything. During the time from the call until I actually knew what had happened, I had to continue to ask God for His peace. The question began running through my mind: "Had someone been injured or killed?" I knew life would never be the same for someone's family, maybe even mine. We found out there had been a normal training flight at night, with five crew members. It ended with the unexpected crash of the aircraft and the loss of all on board. Both companies in the battalion lost men they respected and loved.

With so many within the battalion away for training, it placed a huge responsibility on the unit's Family Readiness Group. I experienced first-hand the resilience of the military spouse. Our hearts were breaking for our friends who had lost their husbands and fathers. We felt the pain of parents who had lost their sons. We immediately volunteered for anything that needed to be done. This was an amazing group of women. As many of us gathered at one of the homes to comfort and support the wife of one fallen soldier, it occurred to me that we had a bond like no other. We were family. Another one of the wives who lost her husband had amazing faith in God. She had been a military spouse for almost twenty years. She was an example to all of us of how to rest in God's peace. She helped us to maintain our focus and continually spoke words of encouragement to us. She reminded us that our husbands loved what they did. They were warriors, serving their nation. I realized that day, nothing I said or did would ever change that!

This event in my life made me realize the tremendous impact we can have in one another's lives. After the tragic news, the spouses rallied and began supporting the five families and their extended families in any way we could. Being in constant contact with these families who were deeply grieving made my faith in God much stronger. When my heart was breaking for my friends, I would pray and God would touch me with His peace. I knew it was real and I could run to Him with whatever circumstances I would face in the future. Hebrews 4:16 became my favorite Bible verse, because it told me to come boldly to the throne of grace so I could obtain mercy and find grace to help me in my time of need. I needed God to help me to be strong so I could help the families in this tragic situation.

Living in the fear of the unknown is no longer unique to special operation families. Today it affects all military families as we face the war on terror. As our family has faced five real-world deployments I have had to ask God to help me not be afraid, but to rest knowing He is my refuge and strength, my help in any trouble (Psalm 46:1-2). It has given me the courage to continue to support my warrior in a job that he absolutely loves.

The second most challenging times of resting have occurred as I have faced unexpected crises while my husband has been deployed. It is during these times I have felt so alone and helpless. One such situation happened in my own life in September 2005. My husband was deployed to Afghanistan. Fort Bragg, North Carolina, had been our new home for a short eight weeks. I was recovering from the birth of our eighth daughter, three weeks prior. It was dinnertime on a Monday evening. The day seemed to be winding down. All of a sudden my nine-year-old daughter came running into the room, yelling, "Ellie cracked her head open!" Impossible, I could not believe what I was hearing. I had been sitting less than ten feet away in our living room while all my girls were in our sun room watching an episode of *Little House on the Prairie*.

Sure enough, as I took my three-year-old into my arms to take a look, I could see that the cut was beyond anything a band aid would handle. After taking a few moments to keep my emotions in check and think through the problem rationally, I realized that our pediatrician was closed for the day. Ugh, this meant a trip to the ER, with a newborn to feed, and no husband. Can anyone relate? Have you noticed when your husband is around that these kinds of things don't happen, or if they do it just doesn't seem like it is a crisis? Lord, thank you for my husband...but back to the crisis at hand.

I will admit I had to keep saying, "Lord, give me your peace! Help me make a plan that will work. How can I take my three-year-old to the ER knowing it will take hours, and still nurse my baby?" Proverbs 2:6 and James 1:5-6 tells us God will give us wisdom! I just had to remember to ask!

I knew the truth in James 1:2-3, which says, "My brethren, count it all joy when you fall into various trials, knowing that the testing of your faith produces patience." I definitely knew I was in the middle of a trial but I was not feeling joyful. I had to keep reminding myself, that it was through times of trial in my life that I had grown closer to God. As I sat in my kitchen I was being watched closely by six pair of eyes waiting to see what I would do. At that moment I realized how I reacted to my situation would be an example to our daughters. If I chose to complain and be angry, that is what they would learn to do in trials. Instead, if I stayed calm and prayed first, they too would learn to maintain their composure and run to God first in difficult situations. The question became, "Was I willing to walk through this trial with God's help, or was I going to rely on my own strength?" It was a matter of trusting God and believing He would help me through it and in the process teach me something new.

As I sat on my kitchen stool, praying, God gave me a calm spirit so I could think and make a plan. I ended up taking my seventeen-year-old daughter with me to the ER. She was old enough to care for my one-month-old as I waited with our three-year-old for care. We actually had to take turns. We were in the ER for five hours. I had to nurse the baby twice as we waited! My seventeen-year-old daughter ended up having to hold her sister as the doctor finished stapling her head, while I was feeding our newborn daughter. God intervened in our situation beyond what I could have thought possible. He provided a wonderful nurse who was also a dad of a three-year-old. The doctor was a quiet-spoken, older woman. Both captured Ellie's trust. It made her care so much easier. As the evening unfolded, God demonstrated His faithfulness by answering my prayers for peace and wisdom. The next morning our three-year-old, Ellie, asked Jesus into her heart because she told me, "Last night I just knew Jesus was with us." God took our trial and used it for good. Would I have chosen a trip to the ER? No way, but God used it to build my and our children's faith in Him.

The other piece of the unexpected seems to only pop up when my husband is gone. My life is full of examples… The A/C in the car died in the middle of the summer, or the time the car didn't run at all. Then there was the time the windows in the house were leaking during a tremendous storm. I realized I needed to get the ladder, crawl onto the roof and quickly clean out the gutters in the midst of the downpour. The lawn mower wouldn't start and the grass was already too long. Or the time during an ice storm when all the electricity went out in the whole neighborhood. I was told it would be at least two or three days before the wires would be repaired. It was fifteen degrees outside and I started chopping wood to keep the fireplace going around the clock. I couldn't feel my nose or my toes. To make matters worse, as I was attempting to chop the wood in blizzard conditions, our oldest daughter, then eight, opened the back door to inform me that I wasn't doing it the way Dad did it!! My personal favorite is the morning I woke up to find the temperature had unexpectedly dropped and our pipes were frozen. I spent the day crawling beneath the house with our Labrador Jesse, covered in spider webs, checking the blow dryer a friend helped me to set up next to the frozen water line. It is during these times and many others like them that my heart struggles to find peace.

Probably the most challenging time in my life came with the birth of our fourth daughter. I know I am not the first military spouse to go through the labor and delivery of a child without their soldier, but it was definitely a test in my own life. I had no time to prepare my heart for my situation. One day I was anticipating, with joy, the birth of our fourth child, only to awaken the next day, wondering how I would be able to do it without my husband. As before, an unexpected mission required my husband to deploy to an unknown place, with an unknown date of return. The cry of my heart was, again, for God's peace and to not be anxious as the birth of our baby drew near. God once again proved He is faithful. Not only did He give me a supernatural peace, but He provided a tremendous support team to help me.

My sister-in-law Mara and her sister Heather asked to come and stay with me through the birth. Mara was to be my labor coach and while we were at the hospital, Heather volunteered to care for and entertain our six children ranging in age from eight weeks to seven years. Once Annie Joy arrived my in-laws and my husband's youngest brother arrived as reinforcements. Our house was full of family and love when I brought Annie home. All of them demonstrated to me the verse that describes laying down one's life for your friends (John 15:13). They put their own lives on hold to serve and take care of me and our family. No matter how impossible the situation seemed, God taught me I could trust Him to provide for my needs no matter the circumstance.

My trials have taught me that God's word is true. As I have faced trials, I have had to continue to pray, letting my requests be known to God with a thankful heart and God has given me His peace. I have claimed the promise in John 14:27 many times over as I have learned to rest. It says, "Peace I leave with you, my peace I give to you; not as the world gives do I give to you. Let not your heart be troubled, neither let it be afraid."

All of these circumstances in my life helped me to grow closer to God as I have chosen to stay calm and rest in His peace and strength (Psalm 29:11). The times I have not I have quickly grown weary and hard hearted, even embittered by my circumstance. This is what happened to me during our time in the 160th Special Operations Aviation Regiment. My husband was gone so much that I began to harden my heart toward him. It was especially hard when my husband was required to be away for what the unit called "planning trips." Occasionally these trips included nice hotel accommodations as well as nice dinners out at local restaurants. I remember one particular trip that caused me to become embittered. Rich was in Miami working at Southern Command. He just happened to call me as I was standing in the commissary parking lot. I had just finished our weekly shopping. It was almost dinnertime and everyone was hungry. I was handing out animal crackers to our four young daughters, while eating a few myself. Rich was so excited to tell me what he was doing, he didn't think to ask me first what we were up to. He began by describing the beautiful sunset he was enjoying while waiting for his lobster dinner to be served. All the while I was continuing to hand out animal crackers, fighting my desire to say something I knew I would regret. Our call ended as his lobster arrived and I never did tell him what we were doing.

The next time my husband had to leave, I had flashbacks of that beautiful sunset and his lobster dinner! My mind allowed me to believe that he enjoyed leaving us. I could feel myself distancing my heart from him. I felt justified as I believed I was protecting my heart from the pain of always having to say goodbye.

We were a few days away from another long separation. This time, my husband was off to six weeks of adventure in Alaska. At least that was the way I saw it in my mind. I didn't consider the hardship he would be facing of maintaining aircraft and completing the training in sub-zero weather. As the time drew near for him to leave, I began to think, "Go ahead and leave, I can take care of our children and home without you!" It sounds ridiculous to me now, but at the time those feelings were real. Eventually he left and my heart grew so hard it made me physically sick. A huge lump formed on my neck. I could not turn my head or swallow without pain. Up until this point in my life, I had rarely gotten sick. I had been a soldier and now I was a long-distance runner and a mother of five children all under the age of ten. These opportunities and challenges in my life had taught me to be physically and mentally strong. It was the first time in my adult life that I was neither. I was both sick and weak. Fear entered my heart as I thought there must be something seriously wrong with me. My fear was for my children. Who would take care of them if something happened to me? I finally went to the doctor and he wanted me to come back for follow-up tests. I never went back because I was too afraid of what they might find. I began to pray for God to heal me. I prayed for God's grace to walk through whatever was to come. It had been six long weeks of constant pain throughout my neck and throat. I went to bed every night crying and praying. One night I was rocking our fifth daughter to sleep, praying fervently for God's peace. Instead of His peace, God began showing me my ugly attitude toward my husband. I began remembering times when I had failed to show him respect in my thoughts, words, and actions. For the first time, I realized how hard and embittered my heart had grown. I began to weep, sitting in the dark, clinging to my baby girl. I immediately asked God to forgive me. I told the Lord how desperately I needed Him to help me change the attitude of my heart. In the moments following my desperate prayer my nose began to run uncontrollably. By the next morning the lump in my neck and the associated pain was completely gone. I believe to this day that my embittered, hard heart caused my body to become physically sick. I also believe asking God to forgive me began the healing process. It was miraculous. I have never been so relieved. This trying time transformed my outlook on this military lifestyle forever. God has helped me to never again become embittered by my current situation or by the separations I had to face in my future. Since that time I have been so grateful to be a military spouse. God gave me the wisdom to understand that my husband didn't enjoy leaving us but it was what he was called to do. He was a soldier. My job was to support him by encouraging him and caring for our family in his absence.

It was painful but the lesson was for a lifetime. Would I choose a life without pain, struggles, and grief and miss God's refining process that has always drawn me closer to Him? These painful times have built my faith. God has never let me down. My faith is what has helped me persevere during the difficult times in this lifestyle. Psalm 66:10-12 reminded me that God does test me. He had placed me in my circumstances and allowed my affliction so He could refine me. In the end He put His finishing touches on my heart that allowed me to love and trust Him more. Never again would I choose to walk through a trial alone and in my own strength. I memorized Isaiah 41:13 which says, "For I, the Lord your God, will hold your right hand, saying to you, 'Fear not, for I will help you.'" This verse became a promise to me. Without conditions God was there to help me!

God allowed me to hear what He was saying to me by using this word picture of holding my right hand because I could relate to it. First, as a wife, if my husband and I are holding hands I feel secure, safe and loved. As a mother I have had many opportunities to hold my little ones' hands.

Our youngest daughter just started walking. When we go outside she wants to do it all by herself but I know I need to help her balance. I don't want her to fall. I say, "Hold Mommy's hand." She reaches up with her little hand and grabs mine. She smiles at me because she feels secure. We start on our walk. She walks with bold confidence because she knows that even if she trips, I will not let her fall to the ground. God showed me this was just like my intimate relationship with Him. He has always been there helping me walk through life with a confidence and peace knowing that He will never let go of me. Psalm 41:10 says it so beautifully! "Fear not, for I am with you; be not dismayed, for I am your God. I will strengthen you, yes, I will help you. I will uphold you with my righteous right hand."

Through my trials as a military spouse, I have learned that the attitude of my heart to seek God for His peace, affected not only my husband, and his ability to do his job, but it impacted our children as well. Even though every parting from my husband is heart wrenching, Rich has told me that he was able to go and do his job because I articulated in both word and deed that I had a peace about where we were as a family and what he was doing as a soldier. He never worried about me creating a separate life for myself and the children. He knew I would continue to support him and include him in our everyday, even when he was away. As for our daughters, except for our youngest, all have surrendered their hearts to the Lord. They have learned to go to God when their hearts are hurting. Our twenty-year-old told me, "Watching you respond through difficult times knowing your heart was hurting, has demonstrated to me that your source of peace is God. By your example, I know Him to be my only source too!"

These years in my life were difficult yet priceless because of how God used them to increase my faith and love for Him.

CHAPTER 9

Maintaining a Place of Refuge

Who can find a virtuous wife? For her worth is far above rubies.

Proverbs 31:10

The heart of her husband safely trusts in her; so he will have no lack of gain.

Proverbs 31:11

Her children rise up and call her blessed: Her husband also and he praises her.

Proverbs 31:28

Love Your Soldier, Love Your Family, Love Yourself

Over the years, as we have moved from house to house, I have continually tried to make our home feel welcoming and look appealing. My husband seldom mentions anything about the physical appearance of our home, but what he does recognize and compliments immediately is what he sees in my actions and attitude. The redecorating my husband notices and appreciates the most is what is coming out of the hidden places of my heart. This "redecorating" happens as I spend countless hours with the Lord allowing His touch to change and transform the places of my heart that need it. The time I devote building and maintaining the foundations of my faith in the Lord is what truly impacts the attitude of my heart as well as the attitude of my family. My foundation of faith is what enables me to be successful at one of the most important jobs I will ever have. That job is to maintain a place of refuge for my soldier and our children.

Most women love to decorate. Whether a small project, such as a birthday cake, or a large one, like changing the color scheme of an entire room, we will invest time putting our special touch on the project and make sure it's just right. My children have told me it is these special touches that have made each house a home. With every move there is a time of cleaning out prior to the packers arriving. My girls remind me each time to not let go of the items that they consider to be part of each home's décor. I remind my daughters that I will not let go of our special keepsakes, but what is most needed as I set up each new home is time spent working on what is in the inner most places of my heart. In Proverbs 14:1, it describes a wise woman as one who builds her house. This house being built in my heart is the time I spend investing in my relationship with God. God clearly tells me unless He builds the house everything I build is done in vain (Proverbs 127:1).

Unique to our role as a military spouse is a family life that requires moving often, separations from those we love, and daily stress and challenges that are associated with this lifestyle. Time has proven that my job to maintain a place of refuge for my soldier and family has been crucial to their welfare. God continues to design and build in my husband and our girls their foundations of faith, but He has allowed me to be their support in the process. Webster's dictionary describes a refuge as a person or thing that gives shelter, help, and comfort. As I have made the commitment to embrace this military lifestyle, God has shown me the importance of my role as the wife of a soldier and mother of military children. The stability I represent makes me the heart of our family, the vital organ needed within the body of our family.

The Bible says, "Where my treasure is, there my heart will be also" (Matthew 6:21). As I surrendered my life as a soldier, no longer did my heart feel torn over what was the most important treasure in my life. Initially, as my role as a wife and mother unfolded, the longing of my heart was to be there for our young daughter.

We had only been in the Army for eight years. Four of those years were spent as a dual military couple. When I was an active-duty soldier, the thought to make our home a place of refuge never crossed my mind. We both were capable, independent, strong soldiers. Everything changed when I held my first baby, Elizabeth, in my arms. The burden I felt to be her refuge altered the course of my life forever. My love for the Army began to grow dim as my love and need to care for her grew with each passing day. Finally, I surrendered my career to stay home with our Elizabeth. Our new assignment took us to Fort Rucker, Alabama. We spent the next two and a half years with no worries, low stress, and a predictable schedule. Family life was very good.

My desire to be a refuge not only for our children but also for my husband became the passion of my heart as Rich was assigned to the 160th Special Operations Aviation Regiment. The picture of our life was totally repainted with our move to Fort Campbell, Kentucky.

My husband was now a special operations aviator, and life held many worries, as my husband was constantly gone flying missions all over the world. His schedule was no longer predictable and the major changes to our lifestyle created new needs within our family. For the first time, I became acutely aware of the needs of assurance, security, trust, stability, peace, and comfort, to name a few. How would I provide for these needs, and why was it important? These were key questions on my mind. The Bible became my "one source" for the answers. I quickly learned that my priorities had to be in order. My commitment to the Lord had to be first in my life, and then love and respect for my husband, followed by a love for my children. This love for my children included a willingness to train them up in the ways of the Lord. This order was essential for me to flourish in my ability to maintain a place of refuge. The goal was twofold, first for my husband and then for our children.

Up until this point in our military lifestyle, my top priority had been for the needs and concerns of our children. After my husband returned from SERE (Survival, Escape, Resistance, Evasion) School, I saw for the first time the significance of his need for a place to find rest, comfort, and the freedom to be real with his emotions. A decision was made in my heart, due to that experience, to invest more time in my husband. It began with my attitude to honor him for who he was, and respect him for what he did. I began to tell him often how proud I was of him. I realized the need to teach our daughters to honor their dad as well. I have seen the fruit of that decision many years later, especially with our teenage daughters. All of our girls absolutely admire and respect their dad. They know he isn't perfect but they show him respect in both word and deed. They tell him often how proud they are of him. More importantly, they take the time to show him their admiration by writing letters and drawing pictures full of words of love and appreciation. In fact, I have a box full of these tokens of love. I am keeping them to share with my husband when we are old and gray.

As my husband began to share his experiences from SERE school, my thoughts were on the environment that I had created to allow him to be real with me. During this particular time, the house was quiet and calm. Our smaller children were napping and I had sent the older girls out to play so we could have a few moments alone. I sat quietly and patiently waiting to hear from my husband. I sincerely wanted to know what he had learned and experienced during the course. The key ingredient to our in-depth conversation was for me to be a good listener. I am an extravert and listening is something I must concentrate on doing. It meant a great deal to me that he was willing to share what he had experienced. Thoughts began popping up in my mind of times when he had communicated very little. Snapshots continued to appear in my mind of the stressful times that I had created. Some of the mistakes I made were taking out my frustrations on my husband for his unpredictable schedule, pressing him for answers for the future, unloading my day on him before giving him the chance to unwind, allowing our children to demand his time before he even took off his uniform, and committing to extra activities without first consulting with him. My lack of communication with my husband and the children caused friction in our home.

My goal became one of creating an atmosphere in our home where someone could share their feelings and be heard. With our large family this goal proved to be a challenge, but I made a commitment that day to strive for a peaceful home. I knew God was the key to making it happen. My husband had already begun daily family devotion time. Our children were being taught what God's word said and we were teaching them how to apply it to their lives. I knew my example as the mother was the foundation for maintaining a peaceful home. I knew if I was not willing to apply God's word to my own actions then neither would our children. My daily attitude would make the difference. I asked God to give me a heart of thankfulness no matter our circumstance. I purposed to thank God every day for my husband and children before crawling out of bed in the morning. My days were so full I made the decision to rise early every day before my family so I could have my much-needed time with the Lord. Isaiah 26:3 says, "You will keep him in perfect peace, whose mind is stayed on You." That decision to begin each day with God has given me the peace I have needed over the last seventeen years. Even in times when I am struggling, God has proven to be my source of help. It has been my faith that has kept me grounded and enabled me to be steadfast and unwavering in this lifestyle. It has allowed me the strength to maintain the place of refuge my husband and children need.

When I asked my husband if he felt like our home was a place of refuge for him, he shocked me with his response of, "not really." I was offended and quickly began to defend all the things I did to make it be so. He put up his hand so I would stop talking and asked that I let him explain. He told me his refuge was being surrounded by all of us. It didn't matter the home we lived in. What was important was the fact that his family was there. Since that time, with each approaching assignment, we have held a family meeting. The response has always been the same. Our priority has been to stay together as a family. No matter the cost.

Right after the devastation of 9/11, my husband's work day was totally unpredictable. He left at 4:00 AM and arrived home after everyone was asleep. It was difficult for our girls, as they were worried about their dad. They knew he was tired and that he would be deploying soon. They longed to see him. It was hard for me to see them carrying such a burden. Harder still was the longing of my heart to help my husband. He was so tired. I wanted so badly to tell him that it was okay to stay in bed for a few more hours so he could get some much-needed rest, but the reality was that there was nothing I could do. I could not change the demands on his life. His country needed and depended on him, just like the countless others wearing the uniform. He would crawl into bed, exhausted. Few words were spoken but we were able to hold hands as we fell asleep. Rich would be sound asleep in minutes. I would lie beside him praying for his health and strength.

Knowing that my husband's schedule wasn't going to change and that he would be deploying soon, I battled thoughts to go home to family where life would have been easier on our children. But I chose to stay. The situation was emotionally draining. Looking back, I know we were my husband's refuge during a very trying time for all of us, especially for my husband. Not only was he working horrendous hours, but he knew he would be leaving us soon.

Our family has lived through many real-world deployments. Having been a soldier, I know it has been much harder on my husband to leave us then it is for us to stay and wait for his return. I realized how many times my husband had been called to leave us and go to serve his nation, in places that were unwelcoming and unfamiliar. Yet, he had done it time and time again without complaining. It allowed me to see the toughest part of leaving to "soldier on" was to leave us, his family. I knew my husband was committed and passionate about his call to be a soldier, but even more so about his call to be a husband and a father. God had given him a soldier's heart to go and accomplish the mission. Realizing this helped me clearly see the priority of my prayers for my husband. He needed prayer to be able to leave us with a heart full of peace. This motivated me to pray for my own strength and peace each time he prepared to leave. I didn't want to break down in tears in front of him or our children. I was determined to send him off with words of love and assurance that we would be okay. Before leaving, I ask my husband to pray for us and then I remind him of our daily prayers for him. This is one of the most important ways our family has maintained a place of refuge for our soldier, even across the miles.

There have been two assignments for my husband that involved only eleven months of schooling. Many people thought it was crazy to uproot our large and growing family and leave the home we had established, simply to be together as a family for a mere eleven months. They thought the better option was for visits over long weekends and holidays. We didn't listen. We didn't care about the difficulty of moving so often. What mattered was our commitment to stay together! Our commitment was put to the test when my husband called from work to tell us he was to command a battalion in Korea. We were shocked. It was the last place we had expected! It meant our second move in eleven months would be overseas. We knew it definitely would have its challenges. The day we received the news, the girls and I had time to discuss our fears and give our concerns to the Lord. We reminded each other of the most important thing: staying together as a family. By the time my husband arrived home that night, God had already begun to transform our hearts and we were talking about the exciting opportunities ahead.

As the weeks went by, feelings began to emerge from our daughters. It was the first time we would uproot a teenager. Our oldest daughter was honest about her struggle to move halfway around the world, away from her closest friends. The younger girls loved our home and the friends they had made in the neighborhood. All were concerned to move so far away from family. As they were honest with me and shared their deepest concerns, I recognized how I had created a place of refuge for them. They were not afraid to be honest with us about the cost to move so far away. This was a new experience for us as parents, but we quickly understood the best thing we could do was to be good listeners. Eventually they came to a conclusion. Having experienced life without Dad many times, they knew it to be hard and definitely no fun. From a biblical perspective, having my husband with us as the leader was the best thing for our whole family. We came to the same conclusion: staying together provided both a refuge and protection for all of us.

Initially, we were told there was no government housing for us in Korea. They said it would be three to four months before any would be available. They encouraged our family to stay in the States and wait. We could have easily made that decision, but instead we chose as a family to travel and to stay together. God provided a small, yet beautiful apartment for us. It was about eight hundred square feet, and at times it felt like we were on top of each other. However, we adapted quickly and we were extremely grateful for our place of refuge in the midst of a new and unusual culture. We had each other and we were experiencing everything together!

The challenge of maintaining a peaceful home became a daily priority in our close quarters. Children who fought, argued, and demanded their way instead of getting along would make a notable difference in the atmosphere of our apartment. A scripture verse that was instrumental to maintaining my goal of a peaceful home was 1 Corinthians 10:24, which says, "Let no one seek his own, but each one the other's well being." It became a memory verse for our daughters. We saw how it impacted their actions and words toward one another and toward us. It also impacted my own life, as a wife and mother. Days where I was tired and weary from the intense schedule reminded me to continue to serve my husband and family. It was my job to look out for their well being. God had proven in my life that His ways work. I knew applying God's word to my situation always changed my attitude. Since then, that particular verse has been fundamental in teaching our children that peace in our home comes when we strive to sacrifice for one another. It was their part in maintaining a place of refuge for their dad and for the rest of the family.

As the wife of a soldier, maintaining a place of refuge for my husband while he is deployed is just as important to me as when he is home. One of the best ways I have found to do this is to keep my heart sensitive to his needs. The keys to my success are praying for him daily and investing in our marriage even while we are apart. I have never wanted to feel like time in our marriage had been erased just because we were not physically in the same location. My goal is always to stay connected. Writing letters is one of my favorite ways to do it. I have found that true feelings flow from my heart through my hands if I will take the time to sit and write. Many times I have read biblically sound books on marriage, all the while asking God to show me areas in our marriage in which I still need to learn and grow. Finally, keeping notes by the phone has helped me to first speak words of encouragement and listen, when my husband has a chance to call. It has also helped me to keep him tuned into "us" even while he is away. I continue to share with him ways he can be praying for us. I purpose to build up my husband, so he can go back to his intense job and do it safely and well.

Recently, my husband and I traveled to Fort Leavenworth, Kansas, for the Pre-Command course. Watching him prepare to leave and upon our arrival, gave me an appreciation for the heart God has put in him to be a soldier. He is so adaptable. He was able to gather his belongings and pack in twenty minutes. It took me over two hours. Within minutes upon our arrival to the place where we would be staying, my husband was unpacked and his computer was up and running. I was witnessing the mindset of a warrior getting ready to accomplish the mission. I was still getting used to the place as it seemed stark, unwelcoming, and certainly unfamiliar to me. My soldier was already prepared to do what was required of him next. I was amazed at the man I was privileged to be married to. He was my hero.

Through my husband's years of service, he has shared the close bonds that have been built among his fellow soldiers. I have recognized these relationships as my husband's refuge while he is deployed. I was able to witness it for myself during my husband's last promotion. He chose to have the ceremony amongst his "band of brothers" in Iraq. The girls and I were able to watch the ceremony over video teleconferencing. The bond formed between the men was evident. My husband's closing remarks spoke of it, and after the ceremony we watched as each man went forward to congratulate my husband. There were many words of encouragement and even a hug or two. All of my selfish desires faded, as I no longer hoped his promotion would be delayed until he returned home. He was promoted among those who understood the honor and responsibility placed upon him. I was so thankful for those men in his life and the bonds of friendship they had formed while fighting for the cause of freedom. When my husband came home, he thanked me. He appreciated my emotional support that allowed him the liberty to be promoted in a war zone in the midst of his fellow soldiers. His words helped me to see I had been a refuge to him because I supported his desire and accepted what I couldn't change.

One of the toughest situations we have lived through happened last summer. My husband had recently returned from Iraq and we had moved to Norfolk, Virginia, where my husband began his last phase of educational training in the Joint Forces Staff College. The six weeks at Fort Bragg prior to moving went smoothly. That all came to a screeching halt a few weeks after arriving in Norfolk, when something unexpected happened. My easy-going, quiet husband turned into a very angry man. My usually calm, even-tempered personality left and I found myself defensive, hurt, and with no control of my temper and tongue. I didn't know what had happened to our wonderful marriage. I didn't recognize my husband and I know he didn't recognize me! I knew my reaction to his anger was like throwing fuel on the fire. It was as if I couldn't control my response to whatever he said. After many weeks of painful, emotional, angry encounters, my oldest daughter finally asked me what was going on between her dad and me. I cried as I said that I didn't know but asked her to pray for me because I certainly wasn't handling the situation the way God would want me to. Soon after, a close friend brought our Mary home from a mission trip. Within a few hours of being in our home, she asked me the very same question. Both times I responded the same way. I believe those verbal confessions began a healing in my own heart, which allowed me to gain control of my tongue. From that day, I prayed desperate prayers for our marriage, asking God to bring healing and peace. I wanted so badly to talk to my husband, but I was afraid of his reaction. We avoided conversation, which was painful to me. God began to show me what being a place of refuge really meant. It was being able to receive the anger and criticism from my husband, during a time when he desperately needed me to be his comfort, help, and shelter. As the Lord healed my heart of anger, He also gave me a heart of compassion for my husband. When I finally worked up the courage to ask my husband what was going on in his heart, God had already been there. Rich was finally able to share some of what was making him angry and frustrated. After many weeks of little communication other than angry outbursts we were able to talk and forgive one another. To this day my husband cannot explain all the anger he was feeling, or the reason why everything I did irritated him, but he knows it was real. Our marriage withstood a very painful time after my husband's return from Iraq. I believe the foundation of faith we both had spent building, prior to finding ourselves in the midst of a fire, is what protected us. My God was already my refuge (Psalm 141:8). Even as I failed to do what was right in His eyes God sustained me through the lonely, misunderstood days, until my husband and I were able to talk. Forgiveness was the means by which God was able to restore our relationship. Now I thank God daily for my marriage and for what He taught me as I ran to Him even when my hurting heart wanted so desperately to run away.

The importance of my job to maintain a place of refuge for my hero was confirmed recently as my husband and I sat on a packed airplane en route to Washington, DC. I was surrounded by people but what caught my attention were the eight sailors scattered in the seats around me. From their conversation, I could tell that they had been away from home for a long time. Our plane was delayed and there was a good possibility they would miss their connecting flight to the west coast. As the minutes went by, one sailor anxiously said, "I just want to get home!" Time stopped for me, as I heard those words over and over in my head. I had heard those same words from my own husband many times over the phone, but I have never seen the look of longing on his face. Watching that sailor announce those words to all who would listen confirmed in my heart what I believed to be true. My faithfulness to maintain a place of refuge for my "man of valor" and our children is truly my priceless profession.

CHAPTER 10
Prayer Warriors

I love the Lord, because He has heard my voice
and my supplications. Because He has inclined His
ear to me, therefore I will call upon Him as long as
I live.

Psalm 116:1-2

Call to Me and I will answer you and show you
great and mighty things, which you do not know.

Jeremiah 33:3

"Lord, teach us to pray." This was the cry of the disciples'
hearts. What had they seen in Jesus' lifestyle of prayer that
inspired them to want it for themselves? The challenges of the
military lifestyle stirred in my own heart the desperate need to
know how to pray. Initially it was motivated by my needs, but
now that desire is motivated by my love for God.

My first recollection of prayer began as a child. I was taught
the Lord's Prayer at a very young age. My mother always
reminded me to say my prayers before going to bed. When I

spent the night with my grandma, she would lie beside me and we would recite the Lord's Prayer together. I grew up going to church and I listened weekly to the pastor as he prayed. I knew God heard his prayers because he was qualified to pray, but what about me? Prayer was a word I heard often but I really didn't understand. I had no idea how God intended for me to use it in my life.

Once, as a teenager, I experienced a time of desperate prayer. My father died unexpectedly when I was sixteen years old. I remember vividly praying to God, asking Him what life was really all about. At that time in my life, I never felt I had heard an answer. Then again at the age of twenty, I said another desperate prayer for safety as I began Airborne School at Fort Benning, Georgia. Within a few hours of arriving to the school I had met a young soldier with a broken leg and collar bone. He had been injured in a jump the week before. It was the first time the thought entered my mind that I could be injured too. Both of these times in my life drove me to pray. I felt helpless, scared, and I knew I was definitely not in control. Praying made me feel better even though I wasn't sure why. My mind was full of questions. I finally began to find the answers at the age of twenty-two when I surrendered all that was in my heart to the Lord. My prayer of surrender included tears from a heart full of anger and bitterness. Thus began my quest to find the answers to the power of prayer and how God used it to transform my human heart.

It was the fall of 1985. I was a young, single second lieutenant beginning Flight School at Fort Rucker, Alabama. Prayer was becoming a part of my everyday life. At this point in my life, I would not have thought of it myself, but God provided exactly what I needed. My first instructor pilot challenged me to pray about everything. He told me prayer was simply talking to God. He set a tremendous example for me, as he prayed before every flight. He did not just recite a memorized prayer. He prayed specifically for the requirements of the day and always for our safety. As I listened to him pray day after day, I realized I was missing something. I listened to him pray with ease and confidence. His example compelled me to ask God to teach me how to really pray. I didn't want to only say prayers from a desperate heart. I wanted to know all I could about prayer. I began searching the Bible and memorizing every verse that had to do with prayer. My understanding of prayer grew with each scripture. Two specific verses that impacted me in a dramatic way were, "Be anxious for nothing, but in everything through prayer and supplication with thanksgiving let your requests be known to God" (Philippians 4:6), and "Rejoice always, and pray without ceasing" (1 Thessalonians 5:16-17). I remember thinking, "God really does want me to pray about everything, all the time!" My part was having the faith to believe that God was listening to me and He wanted to answer my prayers. This was completely different from my traditional saying of the Lord's Prayer at night. I began saying short prayers from my heart. It was like taking baby steps. For the first time in my life, the Lord's Prayer was not the only words I prayed. The more I prayed the easier the words seemed to flow from my heart. Initially my prayer life consisted of always asking God to help ME! Prayers like, "God help me pass this test, help me fly this aircraft well, let me get a passing grade on my check ride." God loved me enough to use these prayers for good, even though they were all self-centered. My understanding of prayer changed one Sunday evening as the youth pastor taught about prayer from Matthew chapter six. He explained verse by verse what Jesus instructions for prayer were to us. Three things he said seemed to be spoken straight to my heart. The first was that God knew my needs before I even asked Him (Matt 6:8), and the most important part of my prayers were words spoken to honor God by recognizing Him as almighty God and praying that His will be done not mine. As my heart received what the scriptures said about prayer I was given a new understanding of how to apply them to my life. God was changing my selfish heart to one of wonder and faith.

I began to pray with a new and genuine faith for specific things going on in my life (James 1:6a). God, in His amazing way, began to reveal Himself to me, through answered prayer.

Two times stand out as God answered my prayers with my new and tender heart during my year at Fort Rucker.

The first happened as I began the Contact phase of flight training. One of the objectives of this phase was to learn to navigate from a helicopter. Navigation required the skill to go from point A to point B, using a terrain map and a compass, while going 90 knots at treetop level. No easy task before the era of global positioning satellites. My stick buddy (my flight training partner) caught on very quickly. He seemed to have no problem following his map. Whenever he navigated for me, we always found our target. Then it would be my turn. I had a great sense of direction on the ground, but in an aircraft going 90 knots, I was a disaster! I was four weeks into an eight-week phase of training and every time I was navigating I continually found myself behind the aircraft while reading the map. I was getting discouraged and was constantly wondering if I would ever catch on. It was the start of the fifth week of training. My stick buddy, once again, navigated flawlessly. Fear to fail again was heavy on my mind. We flew into hot gas, which is refueling the aircraft while it is still running. I was thankful for the break before it was my turn to navigate. As my instructor pilot and stick buddy remained in the aircraft, I jumped out to refuel. As I held the fuel pump, I cried out to God asking Him to please help me navigate. Unlike my previous prayers for help, this time I understood God deserved that I do my very best for His glory. I silently prayed confessing my fear of failing and having to be set back in training. My last words as I hopped back into the aircraft were, "Please help me, Lord!" As we took off, a miraculous thing happened. For the first time, I knew exactly where we were at all times. For over an hour I navigated to every target without a mistake. My flight instructor looked back at me and asked, "What happened to you?" I told him that while I was pumping gas, I was also praying, asking God to help me navigate. He stared at me for a moment and finally said, "It certainly worked!" I remember thinking, "Wow, it really did!" God had heard me and answered my request. I was once again amazed and overwhelmed by the love of God for me. My heart was overjoyed by God's faithfulness to answer my prayers (John 16:24). I couldn't wait to tell the others in my flight class my secret to learning to navigate.

The second prayer was a request for my first duty assignment leaving Fort Rucker. As I shared in my first chapter, this was my husband's idea. He wasn't my husband at the time. In fact, we weren't even engaged! We both had our aspirations and dreams but wanted confirmation that we were to one day be married. We both began to pray for God to assign us to Fort Lewis, Washington, if He wanted us to be husband and wife. I must admit, at the time I really wasn't sure God could answer such a big request. No one was more surprised than I was with the news that we both had been assigned to Fort Lewis following flight school! I was learning that God was faithful to answer my prayers even when I was faithless (2 Timothy 2:13).

These miraculous answers to my prayers became significant milestones in my foundation of faith. A trust was being built in my heart toward God. I wanted to spend more and more time talking to a God who loved me so much. The more I prayed the closer I felt to God even though I did not have all the answers.

I left Fort Rucker for my new assignment to Fort Lewis, Washington. Within a few months Rich and I were married. Life was good! I was doing what I loved to do: fly helicopters and be a soldier, and I was experiencing it with my best friend, my husband. Together as a married couple, we were excited about our future. Life was exciting and fun and I found I wasn't praying as much. I wasn't needy like I had been when I was trying to successfully finish flight school. Now, ten months into our tour at Fort Lewis, I found out that I was unexpectedly pregnant with our first child. I was sick and overwhelmed. I once again began to cry out to God for help. Being a woman and pregnant in a combat arms branch is no easy task! The majority of soldiers I worked with were men. They had no idea what I was feeling. Not even my husband could understand. He had never experienced severe morning sickness. He did not have to put his aviation career on hold for a life that I couldn't even feel or see yet. This was a time in my life when I learned to pour out my deepest thoughts, concerns, and heart issues to God. He in return gave me a comfort and peace that no one else could. As it says in His word, He gave me a peace that surpassed understanding (Philippians 4:7).

Throughout the rest of my pregnancy, the birth of our first daughter, and the next two and a half years serving as a soldier, wife, and mother, prayer became a priority in my life. No longer did I pray because I knew I should. I prayed because it was my connection to God's heart. He had proven His love and faithfulness to me and I knew He always heard me (John11:42). I knew there was no way I was going to be an excellent wife, mother and soldier without the Lord's strength and wisdom. It was through prayer I felt God's leading to give up my career and become a full-time wife and mother.

After praying months over my decision to leave the service, I was beginning to believe God was putting things in my life to teach me how to pray in a deeper way.

As I shared in my first chapter, God answered my prayers to allow me to get out of the military. We left Fort Lewis for Rich to attend the advanced course at Fort Rucker, Alabama. God answered many prayers as I made the transition into my new life as a full-time wife and mother.

My prayers continued daily for help to be a good wife and mom to my growing family. Now four months pregnant with our third daughter, my prayer life took a dramatic turn. My husband had just left for a three-month course at Fort Leavenworth, Kansas. The morning he left I received an unexpected phone call from the OB clinic. They told me to come in as soon as possible. Upon my arrival, I was taken to a room to wait for the nurse practitioner. The nurse practitioner soon came in with the results from my alpha fetal protein test. She told me the test showed our baby to have a neurotube disorder. She quickly explained that babies with such a defect seldom live very long. She then proceeded to tell me the time frame in which I could abort my baby. All of this was spoken to me in a span of five minutes. I was shocked with the news and extremely angry that her only course of action was to end the pregnancy. I demanded to speak with a doctor. During that moment of time as I waited for the doctor, I prayed like I had never prayed before. I wept and cried out to God on behalf of my unborn baby. Eventually, the doctor came to speak with me. He reiterated what the nurse practitioner had said. He gave me the option to fly to Keesler Army Hospital in Mississippi for an amniocentesis, because I would know the results much quicker, or I could retake the blood test. He made sure I understood that the results of the blood work would take longer and that I would not have a lot of time to decide what to do with the pregnancy. I made it very clear that the results would make no difference. We were choosing life for our baby.

This being the age before cell phones, I left the hospital knowing I would not be able to speak to my husband until that evening. Looking back, it was the absolute best scenario for me. Had I been able to contact my husband, I would have poured out my hurting heart to him. Instead, I had to pour out my heart to God, trusting that He was listening.

I already had our car packed in preparation for a planned trip to visit my mom in Wisconsin. My little girls and I left the next day. I had two days of driving ahead of me. I had a lot of time to pray. God was using my situation to teach me how to pray, intercede and truly carry someone else's burden (Galatians 6:2). It just happened to be the burden for my unborn baby! Over the next several weeks, before we received the test results, I continued to pray. One morning as I was running and praying I felt the Lord reveal His heart to me about my unborn child. My thoughts were definitely His thoughts as these words passed through my mind. "Diana, what is considered perfect in the world's eyes is much different than the way my eyes see something as perfect. Trust me with the life of your baby as it is being perfectly designed by Me." I stopped running as my eyes were filled with tears. I stood by the side of the road thanking God for giving me His perspective of the life growing inside of me. My heart changed from one of worry to one full of peace. God's promise of peace that surpasses all understanding began that moment in time to guard my heart and mind (Philippians 4:7). I asked God to help me walk through whatever lay ahead. I knew no matter what happened our baby was being formed exactly the way God intended her to be. I ran home to tell my mom the news. I knew she was extremely worried about me and my baby. I was surprised by her lack of response to my news. We rarely spoke about the baby through the rest of my pregnancy. I knew she must be afraid, and I decided the best thing I could do for her was to pray for her peace and allow her to deal with her emotions about the situation privately. The last appointment before my baby was born they determined the baby was under some stress so they decided to induce the labor.

Prior to this news, my husband and I thought we didn't need any help when the baby arrived. This news changed our minds. We called my mom to ask if she would come to Alabama. She agreed and left Wisconsin almost immediately to drive seventeen hours straight. She was going to be there when we brought our third daughter home from the hospital! The morning we came home she was standing outside as we drove in the driveway. As I opened the van door with our Mary Grace in my arms, my mom without a word reached for her new granddaughter. I stood beside her as she tightly held our beautiful and totally healthy baby girl. I believe in that quiet moment my mom was rejoicing inside with prayers of thanksgiving, just like we had been since the moment Mary Grace was born. I was so grateful God had given me a heart to pray throughout this trial, as I know this gave me strength to not lose heart (Luke 18:1). This time of interceding prayer became another piece in my foundation of faith. The thought never occurred to me but God was using this situation in my life to prepare me for my future.

Eighteen months later we moved to Fort Campbell, Kentucky, with three small children. My husband was beginning his career in the 160th Special Operations Aviation Regiment. I have already shared in my previous chapter on isolation, the very difficult time I had in my husband's initial Green Platoon training. Now that he had successfully completed the training, he was officially a Nightstalker and I was now a Lady Nightstalker. Little did I know how this duty assignment would impact my life forever. This was to be my husband's first assignment to a special operations unit. Operations security was crucial. As a spouse, I attended classes to give me situational awareness as well as to be informed of just how important my silence was to the success of the mission and the safety of our men. We were not to talk with anyone. Not trusted friends, not family members, not even each other. What I had learned about prayer and intercession for my unborn child would now reach a whole new level as I learned to pray daily for our whole family as well as my husband in this new and challenging environment.

Up until this point, Rich had never been assigned to a unit where the intensity of the mission made me concerned for his safety. One of the first requirements upon becoming a Nightstalker was to attend SERE training. It is an intense and very realistic three-week course to prepare a soldier to escape and evade the enemy. The last week is spent as a POW, in a mock POW camp. Having been a soldier, I had heard of the difficulty of the course. The day my husband left began my journey of intercessory prayer for my warrior. I spent the next three weeks praying throughout the day and even throughout the night when I was awake caring for our infant daughter. Prior to this time in our marriage, I had the mentality that my husband was a big boy and could take care of himself. The uncertain and challenging situation he would be placed in gave me a burden for him. He was constantly on my mind and as I thought of him, I prayed for his safety, strength, and morale.

After he returned from SERE school he told me about his time in the mock prison camp. Upon his capture, they placed him into a box and shut him inside. The area was so small that the cover of the lid touched his face. He told me he was extremely uncomfortable but the worst was when they began to play recordings of babies crying. This was the most painful to him, as it reminded him of how much he missed home. He told me that all of the sudden a tremendous peace came over him and he knew I must have been praying for him. He miraculously was able to go to sleep. When I heard his testimony, I had a complete change of heart. For the first time, I realized the power I had through prayer to be a support to my husband. I knew my prayer for him, while he was in SERE training, was heard by God and had made a difference. This gave me a new vision for my role as his wife. One of the most important jobs I now had was to be a prayer warrior for my husband. It did not matter whether he was just working a normal day, gone for training, or out on a real mission, I lifted him up in prayer. When he was home, I would ask him before he left for work how I could be specifically praying for him during his day. While he was away, I prayed for his health and safety and trusted God to take care of the rest of his unknown needs. Rich's SERE training became the catalyst in my life to teach me to pray without ceasing.

Being new to the special operations community, I had little knowledge about what to expect. I knew very little about the intense mission of the unit and how it would impact our lifestyle. I would spend the next five years as a Lady Nightstalker. It was during this time of living in the unknown, waiting for the next mission to arise, and of constantly being separated from my husband that forced me into a lifestyle of prayer. God had placed me right into a situation where He would be the one with whom I would need and talk to the most.

The soldiers and families within the unit were a tightknit community. We did our very best to watch out for and take care of one another. In 1996 my husband was chosen to command one of the companies within the regiment. Once again I became a Family Readiness Group leader. I was thrilled about this opportunity, yet knew in my heart I would need God's help. What I had learned from praying for my unborn daughter and then again from praying daily for my husband became my foundation as the Family Readiness Group leader.

As needs arose, prayer was my starting point. Through all the answered prayers in my own life, God had given me a faith to trust Him for the answers (James 1:6). Any wisdom I had to help and care for the families in the company came straight from His heart. His word told me clearly to just ask for wisdom and He would give it (James 1:5). I had plenty of opportunities to ask with the ever-changing situations as well as the many different personalities within the group. God never let me down. He continually showed Himself faithful. I spent the next eighteen months praying for and investing in a total of one hundred and two soldiers and their families. Supporting my husband's company command in this way was a privilege, but personally, it was one of the most challenging times in my life. The mission was extremely intense. My husband was the commander, which required him to be deployed most of the time. My little girls and I had gotten very spoiled during our previous assignment within a training brigade at Fort Rucker. My husband had never left us in Alabama. Now we were assigned to the most intense aviation regiment in the Army. My husband loved what he did. Every time he left, I felt his excitement to go and lead the best aviators in the world.

As I continued to pray daily for my husband, I began to pray daily for myself and for our young children. I missed my husband, but it was extremely hard to watch the hurting hearts of our three little girls who missed their daddy. I knew I could not be a good mother or an effective Family Readiness Group leader if I was an emotional wreck. I began to fervently pray for God's peace, strength, and wisdom. God provided. My faith was growing as I had to rely on Him more and more. God had placed me in a position where my strength and abilities were no longer enough.

One significant event that happened during this time in my life confirmed my absolute dependence on God. It occurred during the mission to restore democracy in Haiti in September of 1994. Our family was extremely excited as we were anticipating the birth of our fourth child. Unexpectedly, in the middle of the night, my husband's phone rang. He left within the hour and he never came home. I knew the routine. I knew he had been called because of a mission, but this time it was different. This time, I was thirty-eight weeks pregnant! My mind began racing with possible solutions to my situation. Who could help me? I began praying asking God for a solution. This was my first experience with the totally unexpected. Sixteen years later, I now know life as a military spouse is about expecting the unexpected. I finally called my precious sister-in-law, Mara, who was willing to put her life on hold for mine. She brought her three young children including her newborn and came to stay with me until our baby was born. Within a few days, the unit informed us our men were safe and sound. Soon the news was covered with stories about Haiti. U.S. troops were preparing to enter the country by force for Operation Uphold Democracy. I just knew in my heart that was where my husband had gone. Immediately, I began praying for his protection and all who were with him. I couldn't shake the thought of "What if he didn't make it back?" The operational security of the unit required my silence and so my suspicion of where he had gone could only be told to God. I shared my most intimate thoughts and fears with God alone. All of my concerns came pouring out in prayer. How would I react to having my baby without my husband? What would I do if Rich didn't make it back? It was during this time that God became my very best friend. All of my fears drove me to the Lord.

During this time of uncertainty in my life, I prayed with a passion unlike any time before. The more I prayed and laid down my fears before God, the more I felt an overwhelming sense of peace. I came to the place of accepting that whether my husband came home safely or not, God would have to be enough. He had already proven He was the only one who could meet my deepest needs. Those weeks of uncertainty in my life caused me to seek God with all my heart and to not lean on my own understanding (Proverbs 3:5). I now understood why prayer helped. It was my lifeline to God. My prayers were being heard, received, and answered (1 John 5:14-15). With each answer came a desire to talk to God more. It did not matter my circumstance, wherever I was or whatever I found myself preparing to do, prayer became my initial response. God had become my source of help and hope. He continued to reveal Himself to me as I spent more and more time talking to Him.

During these trying years, my faith grew with each situation. God had faithfully answered my prayers. His answers were always the absolute best for the situation and me. To become the prayer warrior God intended me to be, I had to learn many lessons of faith and acquire certain skills. First, I had to choose to pray. Secondly, I had to pray with faith, believing God heard me and expecting Him to answer. Lastly, as I prayed for my children, my husband, and others God put in my life, I had to trust Him with the outcome.

I was beginning to have a deeper understanding of how much God wanted to spend time with me. He loved me. God knew me but He wanted me to know Him as loving and trustworthy. He was using answered prayer to do it. Like a warrior who is given many opportunities to practice his skills and become proficient, God was using events in my life as training ground for me to learn how to pray. Just as a warrior will choose the offensive to protect those in his care I was learning to pray by faith in advance for those in my life. Like a warrior who makes a tremendous difference in any situation he finds himself, God seemed to be teaching me the next skill I needed to impact my circumstances through prayer. A warrior is bold and courageous. Each answered prayer built my confidence and courage to pray more boldly. God was turning my heart into one of a prayer warrior.

As I wrote about this very challenging time in my life, tears filled my eyes. Not only did it bring back how emotionally difficult it was, but the tears were from a heart of thankfulness to a God who used these uncertain times in my life to fill my heart with a love for Him and trust in Him. It built in me a foundation of faith that rejoices in hope, is patient in trials and prays continuously (Romans 12:12). I thank the Lord daily for what He has taught me as I have walked in the shoes of a military spouse.

The circumstances it has placed in my life brought me to the end of myself. There were many times when I could no longer depend on my own strength to get through, but because of answered prayer I found that I could rely on God. My constant need for help and peace made me pray. As a military spouse I have been given many opportunities to learn to pray. They have been endless. The funny thing is the more challenging opportunities seem to repeat themselves. Each set of orders brings the opportunity to pray in preparation for the move and for the desire to start over. Hidden beneath the excitement and adventure of being a part of the military lifestyle are times of prayer when I am lonely, and uncertain of what lies ahead. Prayer has been the key as I have faced the demands and separations of this lifestyle. Just last week I was preparing to say goodbye to my soldier as he was leaving for a one-year unaccompanied tour. At times my heart was hurting so badly I did not dare speak for fear of crying. I was trying to be strong for my husband and our children. I would pray silently asking God for comfort and amazingly a sense of peace would fill me for a moment at a time. It was like the many times I have been unable to speak to my husband because he was deployed. It reminded me I can always talk to God and He quickly hears my prayers and meets my needs when no one else can. This lifestyle demands time in prayer when I need God's strength and wisdom as a geographical single parent and certainly not least the prayers for peace as I wait for my soldier to come home safely. I am so thankful for these many opportunities to learn to pray. Just as a warrior prepares for the day of battle, I have learned I can face each day because my preparation begins with prayer.

Through all the difficult situations in my life, I have learned God's grace was sufficient for me. Through my many times of weakness, God revealed His strength (2 Corinthians 2:9-10). My strength grew as I exercised the powerful weapon God had given me called prayer! Prayer has become my life source of comfort and peace. Being able to draw close to God through prayer is what has sustained me in this lifestyle as the wife of a warrior.

CHAPTER 11
EMBRACING THE MILITARY LIFESTYLE

But as God has distributed to each one, as the Lord has called each one, so let him walk.

1 Corinthians 7:17

"I have chosen you," says the Lord of hosts.

Haggai 2:23

I, therefore, the prisoner of the Lord beseech you to walk worthy of the calling with which you were called.

Ephesians 4:1

When I fell in love with my warrior, I could not fathom how much his profession would impact my world. Little did I know how it would entwine itself around my heart and life. I didn't fully understand the requirement it would place on me, but thankfully God did. God had a plan and placed a call on my life to be a military spouse. The heart of this chapter was written for a dear friend. She was in a place of despair and weariness from the challenges and trials that are common to the military spouse. As I sought to encourage her, I rediscovered the importance of my role as the wife of a warrior.

This revelation has given me a passion to embrace this lifestyle, now more than ever, knowing that God has a purpose for me in it, just as He did for my friend and all who carry the title of military spouse.

A verse that captured my heart is found in the book of Daniel. It says that God rules in the kingdom of men (Daniel 5:21). Knowing I am a part of that kingdom has allowed me to embrace this life God has chosen for me. He has decided my course as I have trusted in Him. The promise in Hebrews 13 says, the Word is the same yesterday, today, and tomorrow. The fact that God's word is unchanging proved to me that God has always been a part of my life. First he gave me a desire to be a soldier. He helped me fulfill that dream and serve my nation for over five years. That experience has given me a deeper understanding into the heart of my warrior. The way my husband leads our family and makes decisions is heavily influenced by his warrior's heart. I believe God knew my army training would be extremely helpful in raising our eight daughters. My training taught me to let go of my wants and desires for a greater cause. This is exactly what is required of me as the mother of eight children. I can also accomplish much on very little sleep. My army training taught me to keep going even when I was extremely tired. Lastly but certainly not least was the training I received in organization and planning.

Thinking ahead is an absolute must in the military as well as in a large family to accomplish any task. Everyone in our family has their chores and each child knows what is expected of them to make our family run smoothly. Each day is an opportunity to continue to train the younger girls to do their part and their very best. Best is not perfect but best is doing their work with a good attitude. Planning and organizing has become a part of the character of each of our daughters. It has paid off every time our family prepares to travel; even our youngest attempts to organize her little bag. She reminds me to not forget her blanket every time we get ready for a trip. I am proud to say the Juergens family has a standard operating procedure in place to move our baseball team plus one anywhere. God has proven over and over how He prepared me to care for our large family as well as be a wife of a soldier. His daily faithfulness assures me He will be there in my future. As I look back, I can see how God used my yesterdays to prepare me for today, and by faith I know as I seek the Lord He will guide me in my future (Proverbs 3:6).

As I read the following passages they emphasize what God's Word has to say to me about the call He has placed on my life. The promises in Psalm 139:13-16 are amazing. To hear how God formed me and in His book, He wrote the days fashioned for me before I was even born, is truly amazing. When I read these verses, it transformed my way of thinking about all that is required of me as a military spouse. Now I am able to embrace what God has for me, knowing He has prepared me for it. By

God's very design He formed and fashioned in me a heart to be flexible and unwavering (Psalms 33:15). This truth has proven itself over and over. The Lord has put in me a heart that can thrive days, months, and even longer without my spouse, a heart that can be both Mom and Dad during separations, a heart that can love my country and serve it by being a part of a military family, a heart of compassion and caring for other military families placed within my sphere of influence, a heart that can plant itself, flourish, and invest in each new duty assignment and yet be able to start all over again with each move, and a heart to love a man whose profession demands that the mission come first! How encouraging it is to know God has prepared me to be a military spouse.

I once read the words of a military spouse who referred to the military as a hard life. Her attitude was to just deal with it. I remembering thinking, "I refuse to just deal with it. I want to make the most of it!" It hasn't always been easy, but understanding the fact that the needs of the military must come before me and our family has helped me with my attitude during the difficult times when the mission demanded the presence of my soldier even when there were special needs at home. My husband's profession demands that he be available 24/7 for the cause of freedom. I cannot change the hours he is needed to work, the responsibilities placed upon him, or the number of deployments he will be required to participate in. My husband chose to wear the military uniform and in his contract, on the line below the words, "I swear to defend and protect the constitution of the United States against all enemies, foreign or domestic, so help me God," he signed his name! At that point in time, he made a commitment to his country, before all else in his life.

I was very encouraged after reading two books portraying the lives of Ike and Mamie Eisenhower as a military couple. Both had personal testimonies of the challenging demands on the military spouse. The example from Mamie's life that impacted me the most began a few days after marrying her young soldier. She followed her new husband to Fort Sam Houston, Texas. They had been there less than a month when he told her he would be leaving her for several weeks of training. Being a new military wife, she was shocked. She was not ready for him to leave her all alone. I found it comforting to read her reaction to the same true fact: a soldier's country must come first and his family second.

One advantage I have had over the years was the understanding gained from having been a soldier myself. I know firsthand that the mission has to come first. It has been my day-to-day response to this fact that has made the difference in my life. I must constantly examine the attitude of my heart. How I respond to the demands placed on my soldier's life impacts not only me, but my husband and our family as well. When my husband is not deployed one of our goals as a family is to have dinner together. Throughout my husband's career this has not been easy due to his long workday. Because it is important to us, I choose to feed the children a snack at 5:00 PM and plan dinner for 7:30 PM. While we wait for Dad to come home I give early baths and have the children ready to hang out with him for a few minutes after dinner. I have not always been crazy about cleaning up the kitchen at 8:30 at night, but it has paid off. When my husband is home, he has been able to look his children in the eyes and discern all is okay. I could have chosen the easier path and served dinner to our children at a normal hour and let my husband eat alone. Instead I chose to work our schedule around his. Over the years, our daughters have watched and learned from my example to either embrace the challenges of this lifestyle by being creative or become embittered by them. This is a daily choice that I must make.

I believe my husband was created by God to be able to do what he does, just as I believe I was created to be his help meet in my role as a military spouse. It has been a privilege to be married to such a man of integrity. I am so proud to be married to such a selfless, courageous man. He is a "man of valor" as God describes Gideon in Judges 6. He has the heart of a soldier. Understanding this about my husband has truly helped me to support him in any way I can. This is his chosen profession…the calling placed on his life. When the phone rings and the family plans must change due to the mission, we have learned to go on, making the most of our situation. When he comes home from a long day or deployment and talks to me like one of his soldiers, I have learned to smile and remind him he is home!

This lifestyle can be extremely hard, but I refuse to deal with it and just survive. I want to embrace the call on my life as a military spouse knowing if I don't it will negatively impact my husband and my family.

Isaiah 55:3 says, "Give ear and come to me; hear me that your soul may live." I have learned over the last twenty-one years that if I listen to God, apply His word to my life, and give Him all my cares and concerns, He will give me what I need to thrive and grow and to not feel defeated in this lifestyle.

The difficult times have forced me to revisit some important questions. Did I want to call it quits? No way! Did I really want my soldier to get out of the military? Absolutely not! Then I must answer the next set of important questions. Do I believe God knows our every circumstance? Has God proven He will sustain us and teach us through every difficult situation? Had God been faithful to provide support and help when we were in need? It was a resounding "yes" to all three questions. Once again, my attitude was transformed in the midst my trial and I was determined to thrive, not merely survive.

I began to study the scriptures to show me God's heart. What I found was solid evidence that my role as a military spouse was a call placed on my life by the living God! Beginning with Hebrews 12:1–2, "Therefore we also, since we are surrounded by so great a cloud of witnesses, let us lay aside every weight, and the sin which so easily ensnares us, and let us run with endurance the race that is set before us, looking unto Jesus, the author and finisher of our faith." I likened my role as a military spouse to the race. God was using this lifestyle to mold me into the person He wanted me to be. The key to running the race with success was choosing Jesus as my source of strength, peace, and joy.

Verse one speaks of running with endurance the race that is set before us. The dictionary defines endurance as the act, fact, or power of bearing up under hardships or difficulties, such as pain, stress, or fatigue. The dictionary uses the example of a long-distance runner who must have endurance. As a marathon runner, I could relate to the truth in this statement. In those last six miles of a marathon there is pain and fatigue involved, even with the proper training, at the end of the race it is the attitude of my heart to not give up that pushes my body across that finish line. In 2004, I ran the Suwon Marathon in Suwon, South Korea. To date it is still the most challenging course I have ever run. It was extremely hilly. We ran much of the course beside the unending traffic of South Korea. The temperatures unexpectedly soared into the nineties and our only source of hydration came in the form of sponges soaked with water. As the last miles approached I felt I just needed a word of encouragement. There were none to be had as I was only one of four Americans in the race. I wasn't sure who else could speak English so I didn't attempt sparking up a conversation with any of the other runners. The thoughts to quit first entered my mind as a very old Korean woman passed me at mile eighteen. As I battled the thoughts to quit, it was the Lord who brought the word of encouragement I truly needed. In those last miles I had been searching for a person to talk to and yet because of God's great love for me, He spoke to my heart and reminded me I was not alone because He was with me. He was my source of strength to finish, not other people. It encouraged me to finish what I had started. My attitude was totally changed as I remembered I had decided to run the marathon. No one had forced me. It was a tremendous lesson to learn as I applied it to my call as a military spouse. I chose to marry a soldier. No one forced me. Like the unexpected in the marathon there are many times the unexpected happens in this lifestyle. Remembering I am not alone and guarding my attitude is what has enabled me to not give up but to keep involved and pressing on to thrive as my husband soldiers on. God knew what He was saying when he used the analogy of running a race to describe the call on my life to follow Him. He has chosen that I follow in this lifestyle as a military spouse. When I think of running, I know it will be work, and it will not be easy. I know there is action involved on my part, I am not just waiting for something to happen, but instead actively involved, and as a runner in a race, I must be moving forward! God's heart for my life is that I continue to grow and to move forward in my faith as I keep my eyes on Him! He knew this call to be a military spouse would not be a life of ease. When I read the definition of endurance, bearing up under hardships or difficulties, I thought, "Wow, they could use these same words as one of the definitions for a military spouse."

The definition of enduring sparked thoughts of my journey. A flood of memories came rushing back in my mind of the number of hardships and difficulties we had truly been through because we embraced our role as a military family. I considered just a few, the demanding schedules, painful goodbyes, starting over with each new assignment and the emotional roller coaster of life without our soldier due to a deployment or unaccompanied tour. Just like every other military spouse on the planet, I can make a list of times I have longed for my husband's presence. My husband missed the arrival of our fourth baby girl. He has missed birthdays, anniversaries, and many other special events. That is why the verses in Hebrews spoke to me. God was reminding me to run with endurance the race He had chosen for me and our family. It wasn't that my husband has wanted to miss any of these special events, and it was equally difficult for him to not be present, but the call on his life to be a soldier demands the mission to come first. This is what is required of us as a military family. Through it all, God has been teaching me to keep my eyes on Jesus, the author of my book of faith. God's word continually encourages me to not become weary and discouraged. In this lifestyle, there are definitely times of weariness, especially in the middle of a deployment. It is easy to grow weary from the weight of carrying the load of training children and caring for the home. Feeling at times that there are not enough hours in the day to get everything done! Especially difficult for our family is that time around dinner, when we wish our favorite person in the world would walk through the door. As a mom I look forward to a father's perspective to situations that have popped up during the day as well as another set of helping hands. This time of day is the hardest for me as it reminds me daily the heaviness in my heart of missing my husband.

This is when I must decide. Am I going to be discouraged and wish away each day to just get it over with? Am I going to just get through a particular assignment or deployment or am I going to make the best of it? I have tried both ways, and choosing the latter is the only option! I have chosen to believe the promise of what God says in Hebrews 13:5, "Let your conduct be without covetousness, be content with such things as you have, for the Lord himself has said, 'I will never leave you, nor forsake you.'" It has been a word of encouragement to me as well as our children. No matter how weary I may feel, God is still with me! This has brought comfort and strength to me during these years as the wife of a soldier. God knew what would be required of me and of our children.

I know God has chosen this lifestyle for me! 1 Corinthians 7:17 says, "But as God has distributed to each one, as the Lord has called each one, so let him walk." This verse encourages me daily to embrace my role as a military spouse. It begins with guarding my heart with all diligence, for out of my heart spring the issues of life (Proverbs 4:23). In our house those issues affect nine other people, especially my warrior. My ability to embrace the role God has given me begins in my heart. My husband and our children are watching me to see how I will respond to each situation. They will know by my words and actions if my heart is sincere. I was truly put to the test in the summer of 2005 as we arrived in Fayetteville, North Carolina. I was seven and a half months pregnant with our eighth daughter, Olivia. We had just come home from two years in Korea. We felt we had plenty of time to move in and get settled before the baby would be born. This was very important as we had chosen to have our baby at home, under the watchful care of a nurse midwife and surrounded by the love of sisters. Unfortunately as the days went by our household goods from Korea still had not made it to the States. I began to get somewhat anxious as our bed was in the delayed shipment. I really wanted to deliver our new bundle of joy in the peaceful and quiet setting of our bedroom. Finally we received the call that our household items would be delivered. It just happened to be one day after our baby was due. It was the night before our household goods were to arrive. I was certain I had achieved my goal of the delivery of the household goods prior to the delivery of my baby. It was 9:00 PM and I had just finished reading to our little girls and put them to bed. I was brushing my teeth when I experienced the first contraction. I looked in the mirror and said, "Not yet, Lord." I was in complete denial until my husband saw my face as I experienced a second contraction. He always gets excited as the onset of labor begins. This night was no different even though I told him I wasn't ready! He assured me everything would be fine. This has become a tremendous story of faith in our home because once again God was there to provide my every need. God provided a fabulous midwife and doula. A doula is trained to be the moral support to the one in labor. Doris Ann had never been to a home birth but asked if she could come to mine. She arrived before the midwife with a heart full of encouragement and a big, soft birthing ball. The ball was just the right size for me to sit on so I could rest between contractions. It completely took the place of my missing comfortable bed! Our three oldest daughters asked to be present for the birth and they became my prayer warriors as well as great assistants to their dad as he helped me through each contraction. I often laugh about this situation but tell my husband my ability to calmly walk through that unusual circumstance, brought on by this military lifestyle, should prove my loyalty and heart to support him, no matter the cost.

As I embrace this call on my life, I can trust God with every circumstance because I have learned He will use them to increase my faith and in some way make a positive difference. In the days leading up to and during the birth of our Olivia our daughters were watching me. They saw me go through that experience without complaining but instead thanking God for the spirit of flexibility He had given me to be a military spouse.

Most importantly, as I have embraced this lifestyle, I have encouraged our children to do the same. I have told them of the important role God has placed on their lives to support their dad. The evidence of their support has been seen in their willingness to move even as they are leaving precious friends and to not complain as we begin again at each new assignment. God has shown them He cares by answering their prayers for new friendships and opportunities they never dreamed of in each new place. The most powerful example of how they have truly embraced this lifestyle happened as they heard the news of their dad's upcoming assignment. He had already been chosen for a brigade command, and our daughters were thrilled at the thought of being able to serve soldiers and their families once again. Then the unexpected news arrived via a phone call from my husband while he was deployed to Iraq. He told me he had been chosen to command in Honduras. It meant a one-year separation for our family. He asked me to not tell the children and we would have a family meeting when he got home. I hung up the phone and thanked the Lord for helping me control my emotions. I had many weeks to pray before that meeting took place. A few days after the emotional homecoming, my husband called our family to the table. He began by telling us that he loved what he did but that we were his pride and joy. He went on to tell of the command in Honduras. The girls were amazingly calm. I knew it was because I had prayed in advance for their hearts' reaction as well as my own. God answered those prayers in an amazing way. My husband went on to ask our girls if they thought he should take the command. I was so proud of my husband that day. Not just because he had been chosen to command but because of his father's heart. He was willing to give up his desire to command because of his concern for our needs and love for our family. Within a few minutes, those old enough to understand the cost were saying yes. They told their dad they would not like being apart but God had ultimately decided. I was so humbled by their faith to trust God with our future. I also saw how their dad's profession had entwined itself around their hearts too.

God brought the story of Esther to my mind as a wonderful example of how I can truly trust Him with our future. Esther was a beautiful Jewish girl. In her day, the king, who ruled all of the land from India to Ethiopia, sent his wife away, because she disobeyed. This king soon realized that he missed his wife. The king's servants came up with an idea. They convinced the king to let them go into all the land to gather all the beautiful young women and bring them to the palace. He then could choose a new wife. The king agreed and Esther became one of the young women chosen to go.

Esther had to leave her family and all she knew because an authority greater than herself said so. In my own life that authority is the call on my husband's life to be a soldier in the

U.S. Army. Esther's situation was comparable to my own as she was taken to a strange and unfamiliar place. She had to find her way and make new friends. I found myself remembering similar circumstances in my own life with each new set of orders.

Eventually, Esther was chosen to be the new queen. Due to bad information and the influence of an evil man, her husband, the king, decided to destroy her people, the Jews. God had placed Esther in a perfect position to influence his actions and change his mind. It made me think of the assignments I would not have chosen, yet those were the exact ones through which God allowed me and our family to make a remarkable difference in the lives of our neighbors, families within the military and in our community.

It confirmed in my heart God knew exactly what He was doing. God had placed Esther into these circumstances because that is exactly where He needed her. Her uncle sent word to her, telling her that she must take action to save her people, the Jews. I remind myself often of the challenges Esther had to face. She was taken from her home and everything that was familiar to her. She initially did not want to leave her family and friends. The Bible tells us Esther was afraid. She was separated from her loved ones and unsure of what was in her future. Very much like the lifestyle of the military spouse.

Even with Esther's example to follow, I have not always embraced the news of unexpected change. When I first heard we were moving to Fort Bragg, North Carolina, I acted like my three-year-old, who at the time kicked and dragged her feet whenever she did not want to do something. I did not want to move to Fort Bragg; I wanted to move to Germany.

I had joined the military in 1985, with a dream to serve in Europe. I resigned before I had the chance, but I had married a soldier. I felt certain one day the opportunity to be stationed in Europe would present itself. It finally did. As our tour in Korea was coming to a close, my husband was offered a position in Germany. Needless to say, I was thrilled until a few weeks later when my husband was asked for, by name, to work at Fort Bragg. I was so disappointed. I even asked God why the plan had to change.

Looking back at how the story of Esther ended, it was the key verse of Esther 4:14 that completely transformed my negative attitude about our assignment to Ft Bragg. Esther's uncle challenged Esther with these words when she was unsure and afraid, "Yet who knows whether you have come to the kingdom for such a time as this?" When Esther heard these words, she realized she didn't know the outcome but that she must trust God and act. She approached the king, and she saved her people from destruction! I also had to trust and act as I decided to embrace whatever God had decided for our family at Fort Bragg. Our time at Fort Bragg was not easy but it turned out to be one of the best assignments for our whole family. We grew in our faith and made lifelong friends.

Esther's example to embrace what God had for her continues to transform the way I respond to another set of orders to move again, or another deployment. Even something much simpler, such as those times when the unit's Family Readiness Group is looking for volunteers. I want to be willing to sacrifice my heart's desires and my time to support my warrior, my family, and others.

Esther had no idea about the changes that were coming into her life, but God did! We are now approaching our first unaccompanied tour and, like Esther, we are trusting God with the outcome, knowing He has decided this for our family. We believe He is placing us where He needs us, where we can make a positive difference, and where He knows we will adapt and grow the most!

I know God has called me and equipped me to thrive in this lifestyle as I support and serve my warrior, my family, and ultimately our nation. What a difference it makes in my attitude to fully understand that God has chosen me, and created me to be a military spouse! My hope is to continue to embrace this call on my life with joy, trusting God with my whole heart for the outcome!

CPSIA information can be obtained at www.ICGtesting.com
Printed in the USA
BVOW07s1919170813

328693BV00001B/23/P

9 781606 100066